# Leslie Fiedler

## Twayne's United States Authors Series

Warren French, Editor

*Indiana University, Indianapolis*

TUSAS 492

LESLIE FIEDLER
(1917–      )
*Photograph courtesy of Leslie Fiedler*

# Leslie Fiedler

## By Mark Royden Winchell

*Clemson University*

*Twayne Publishers • Boston*

*For Jim, Sally, and Shelli Li Calland*

*Leslie Fiedler*

Mark Royden Winchell

Copyright © 1985 by G.K. Hall & Company
All Rights Reserved
Published by Twayne Publishers
A Division of G.K. Hall & Company
70 Lincoln Street
Boston, Massachusetts 02111

Book Production by Elizabeth Todesco
Book Design by Barbara Anderson

Printed on permanent/durable acid-free
paper and bound in the United States of
America.

**Library of Congress Cataloging in Publication Data**

Winchell, Mark Royden, 1948–
  Leslie Fiedler.

  (Twayne's United States authors series; TUSAS 492)
  Bibliography: p. 158
  Includes index.
    1. Fiedler, Leslie A.—Criticism and interpretation.
  2. Criticism—United States.  I. Title.  II. Series.
  PS3556.I34Z94  1985        810'.9        85–8734
  ISBN 0–8057–7451–3

# Contents

# *About the Author*

Mark Royden Winchell has published essays, reviews, and poems in such journals as the *Sewanee Review*, the *American Spectator*, *Chronicles of Culture*, the *Canadian Review of American Studies*, the *Mississippi Quarterly*, the *Ohio Journal*, *Christianity and Literature*, the *University Bookman*, the *Southern Humanities Review*, *Western American Literature*, the *New Oxford Review*, *Literature and Belief*, the *South Central Bulletin*, *Resources for American Literary Study*, and the *Journal of Country Music*. In addition, he has contributed to several books, including *A History of Southern Literature*, *Los Angeles in Fiction*, *Contemporary Literary Criticism*, *Literature of Tennessee*, *Modern American Fiction: Form and Function*, *Shakespeare and Southern Writers: A Study in Influence,* and the third edition of William Rose Benet's *Reader's Encyclopedia.* His major publications are studies of Joan Didion and William F. Buckley, Jr., in Twayne's United States Authors Series, monographs on Horace McCoy and John Gregory Dunne in the Boise State University Western Writers Series, and a special issue of the *Southern Quarterly* entitled *Country Music: Tradition and the Individual Talent.* At present, he is coediting a collection of essays on Vanderbilt writers. Winchell holds the B.A. and M.A. degrees from West Virginia University and the Ph.D. from Vanderbilt. He is currently associate professor of English at Clemson University.

# Preface

In 1963 the British critic Ronald Bryden wrote: "Leslie Fiedler is probably known to English readers as the man who defended the Rosenbergs' execution, stuck up for McCarthy as the heir to William Jennings Bryan's corncob throne and accused Huckleberry Finn of being a nigger-loving liberal homosexual."[1] The fact that Fiedler did none of those things (something that Bryden readily concedes) suggests that there is a considerable gap between the man's reputation for outrageousness and the actual dialectics of his thought. It is the reputation that has made Fiedler interesting enough to warrant a book-length study, but his genuine achievement that makes such a study more than a mere exercise in sensationalism.

As the author of more than twenty books and hundreds of essays, Fiedler poses a challenge to anyone seeking a complete assessment of his role in contemporary literature. I have therefore had to make some hard choices in regard to emphasis. The focus of certain chapters in this study should be immediately apparent: chapter 1 is concerned with Fiedler's life; chapter 5 with his masterpiece, *Love and Death in the American Novel;* chapter 7 with his "Jewish essays"; chapter 11 with his work on Dante and Shakespeare; chapter 12 with his fiction; and chapter 13 with his writings on nonliterary topics (chapter 14 is a general conclusion). This still leaves a considerable body of work that I have chosen to deal with thematically.

Chapters 2–4 concentrate on a few "typological" essays that lay the groundwork for much of Fiedler's thought. These include the frequently anthologized myth manifestos "In the Beginning Was the Word" and "Archetype and Signature" (chapter 2) and the less well known *"Chutzpah* and *Pudeur"* (along with "Caliban or Hamlet," a variation on the same theme) and "The Eye of Innocence" (chapter 3). Chapter 4 rounds out this discussion by examining the more conventional typologies of place and time. Chapter 6 serves as a sequel to my analysis of *Love and Death in the American Novel* by bringing together Fiedler's treatment of Indians in *The Return of the Vanishing American* and blacks in "The Inadvertent Epic" (a concept developed at length in the second section of *What Was Literature?*). The final series of "thematic" chapters (8–10) looks at one of the continuing preoccupations of Fiedler's career—the opening of the literary canon to popular culture.

Since virtually no one (not even Fiedler himself) agrees with everything that Fiedler has written, I do not expect everyone to agree with what I have to say about him. However, I hope that I have discussed the relevant issues with sufficient clarity that all disagreement will be informed and intelligent. Finally, there is something to be said for having a synoptic overview of a career as various as Fiedler's. As Emerson noted: "the integrity of impression made by manifold natural objects . . . distinguishes the stick of timber of the woodcutter from the tree of the poet."[2]

Mark Royden Winchell

*Clemson University*

# Acknowledgments

I am pleased to acknowledge several persons who have assisted me in the preparation of this book. Leslie Fiedler and his secretary Joyce Troy have been prompt and courteous in answering questions and providing me with resources that would otherwise have been difficult to obtain. In addition, Professor Fiedler has granted me permission to quote from his published work. William J. Studer and A. Robert Thorson have once again granted me use of the Ohio State University libraries. Karen Kozak has graciously shared the fruits of her bibliographical research, and Beverly Broome has provided important technical service. James Calland, Betsy Dendy, and Joycelyn Trigg have read and commented on much of the manuscript, and my parents have given me a haven in which to work with minimal distraction. Finally, I thank Warren French for believing in this project and helping to see it through every step of the way.

# Chronology

1967   Arrested on drug charges.

1968   *The Return of the Vanishing American.*

1969   *Being Busted* and *Nude Croquet and Other Stories.*

1971   *The Collected Essays.*

1972   Drug conviction reversed. *The Stranger in Shakespeare.*

1973   Divorces Margaret Shipley. Marries Sally Smith Andersen.

1974   *The Messengers Will Come No More.*

1975   *In Dreams Awake.*

1977   *The Fiedler Reader.*

1978   *Freaks: Myths and Images of the Secret Self.*

1981   *English Literature: Opening Up the Canon* (with Houston A. Baker, Jr.).

1982   *What Was Literature?*

1983   *Olaf Stapledon: A Man Divided.*

# Chapter One
# Dr. Lusty Fiddler

I was introduced to Leslie Fiedler's criticism during my first semester as an undergraduate English major. However, it was not until thirteen years later that I actually met him. He was speaking, appropriately enough, at my alma mater, West Virginia University. With white hair and beard, an obvious love of good food and drink, the ever-present cigar, and a gleam in his eye that was halfway between a twinkle and a leer, he looked for all the world like Kris Kringle playing the dirtiest beast of the age.[1] The subject of his talk was *The Birth of a Nation* and *Gone With the Wind,* and afterward he showed up for the brie and chablis bash in the basement of an off-campus dormitory. Among those who gathered around him were the usual mix of well-wishers, groupies, and gadflies, looking for everything from an autograph to an argument. I suspect, though, that he was most pleased by those who simply wanted to share their enthusiasm for our popular culture (*The Godfather, Tarzan of the Apes, Hill Street Blues,* and all the rest). "Who is this Leslie Fiedler?" asked a legendary-local-rock-singer-of-the-sixties-since-fallen-onto-hard-times. "Why man," replied a legendary-local-bohemian-of-the-sixties-since-fallen-into-hospital-administration, "He's a famous myth guru."

## Disturbing the Peace

Waking up on the morning of 29 April 1967, Leslie Fiedler was greeted by the following headline in the Buffalo *Courier Express:* "UB Professor, Wife, Son, Arrested on Dope Charges." Beneath were pictures of the three offenders and a story informing readers that "Dr. Leslie A. Fiedler, a University of Buffalo English professor and novelist, his wife, their son and daughter-in-law were among six persons arrested on narcotics charges Friday night in the Fiedler home. . . . Dr. Fiedler, 50, author of four novels and faculty adviser to LEMAR, a U.B. student organization which advocates legislation [*sic*] of marijuana, was charged with maintaining premises where narcotics are used. . . . Police had kept the Fiedler residence under 24-hour surveillance for the last 10 days."[2]

When the story reached *Time,* it had been embellished to state that Fiedler "was arrested in his home during a pot-and-hashish party" (see *BB,* 126). The facts, however, were a bit more mundane. Although *Time* managed to get the name of SUNY-Buffalo right (the old University of Buffalo had several years earlier been absorbed into the state university system), the "pot-and-hashish party" was a total fabrication. Fiedler and his wife were preparing to go to the movies with a son and daughter-in-law, while a second son, "far from engaging in some wild orgy, happened to be in the process of taking a bath" (*BB,* 139). It was at that inauspicious moment that several policemen entered the Fiedler home, without having knocked, screaming "We knocked! We knocked!" (*BB,* 130).

Five minutes later the police were able to produce a warrant, sworn out by a homeless seventeen-year-old girl who had been be-friended by Fiedler's wife and daughter. This pathetic waif had been recruited by the police to enter the Fiedler home with a concealed listening device (which was monitored from a bread truck across the street) and—according to Fiedler—to plant marijuana on the premises. Perhaps the ultimate indignity had occurred when this young "friend" (with her concealed listening device) had shared wine and unleavened bread with the Fiedlers at their Passover seder. Remembering that evening, Fiedler writes:

The ironies are archetypal to the point of obviousness (one of my sons claims we were thirteen at table, but this I refuse to admit to myself), embarrassingly so. I prefer to reflect on the cops at their listening post (in the bread van?) hearing the ancient prayers: "Not in one generation alone have they risen against us, but in every generation. . . . This year we are slaves, next year we shall be free!" I cannot resist reporting, however, that at the end of the evening, the electronically equipped "friend" said to me breathlessly, "Oh, Professor, thank you. This is only the second religious ceremony I ever attended in my life." (My wife has told me since that the first was the lighting of Channukah candles at our house.) (*BB,* 137)

This troublesome farce (which eventually cost Fiedler an insurance policy, his Diner's Club card, and $20,000 in legal fees) is not only the best-known incident of his life, but an absurd parable for that life. Caught supporting the wrong side of the generation gap in a blue-collar community at a critical period in the sixties, Leslie Fiedler was persecuted not because of what he did, but because of what he was—or what he was believed to be. Many of the good citizens of Buffalo would have told you that he was a pot-smoking Communist professor. And yet he did not smoke pot, had long since become disillusioned with the Soviet Union, and has never been comfortable in the pontifical role of professor. Such misunderstandings have plagued Fiedler for his entire career and will probably continue to do so as long as he cherishes the role of barbarian and disturber of the peace. It was a role that he began to play as a radical adolescent on Newark's Bergen Street over fifty years ago.

Born in the same year as the Russian Revolution, Leslie Aaron Fiedler came of age during the 1930s. Years later, he would recall: "at 15 I had the sense of being in full possession of everything I could need for doing what I imagined I wanted to do in life. . . . I was growing up in a time when it wasn't possible to relish youth or play 'being young.' "[3] (Fiedler is only one of many who see his later life as an act of compensation for this lack of childhood.) Although he went through the Newark school system, his real education was gleaned from reading books at the public library and attending various radical meetings. He remembers "the books on the open shelves of the library, the bums and hoboes in the Park eager to tell lies to one young enough to believe them, the street-corner speakers yelling over the hecklers." All of these suggested to him "the difficulty and allure of communication, created for me an image of the writer-speaker (even what I write for print is silent speech) trying to be heard over the roar of traffic and the whispered jokes of a hostile audience."[4]

Because Newark was what we now euphemistically call a "changing community," the complex social relations between Jews and blacks (only recently become a matter of national interest) was part of the fabric of Fiedler's early life. When he was little more than a year old, he was taken care of by a black girl to whom he was so attached that he horrified his family by caressing and kissing her alien skin. (The girl was promptly fired.) Later he remembers walking to school through a neighborhood largely populated by hostile blacks and Jewish gangsters (one of the more successful of the latter ran a free soup kitchen throughout the depression). Although he was himself a staunch believer in racial equality, he recalls that for others in this neighborhood "a standard way of proving one's tough-ness was 'nigger smashing.' This sport involved cruising a side street at a high rate of speed, catching a lonely Negro, beating the hell out of him and getting back into the car and away before his friends could gather to retaliate" (CE, 1:468).

Because his ambition was to spend his life talking about the books he loved, Fiedler began commuting by bus, ferry, train, and subway to New York University, where he pursued a degree in literature. There, in lieu of freshman themes on "How I Tie My Shoes," he wrote surrealistic stories while riding the Lexington Avenue subway. One dealt with "the strange life and death of a woman who had an orgasm every time she passed through a subway turnstile." Another "concerned a man who married a seal but was unable to find a way to consummate their union and perished (along with his bride) of sheer frustration." Unfortunately, "the latter was a translation only and lacked the real point of an original version which I had composed in uncertain French—after I had discovered that the French word for seal was *phoque*" (CE, 2:358). One of his most vivid memories of those years was of a large Italian boy who drove a truck all night, slept in class all day, and once stormed out of a biology lecture because "he could not abide being taught natural science by a virgin" (CE, 2:360).

After completing his B.A. at NYU in 1938, Fiedler entered the University of Wisconsin, where he took his M.A. in 1939 and his Ph.D. in 1941 (his dissertation topic was "John Donne's *Songs and Sonnets*: A Reinterpretation in Light of Their Traditional Back-grounds"). At this point, he continued his journey west (or as he prefers to call it, his "flight from the East") by accepting a position at Montana State University. As Hugh Kenner imagines it, "In '41, straitjacketed in his new doctorate, the burly Fiedler was bundled by implacable Fate into the train that would haul him off kicking and fuming to the academic Gulag in Montana. Folklore has cher-ished and doubtless improved the scene at his departure: the sighs of commiseration on the platform, the indomitable leonine head at the coach window, its defiant shout through roars of escaping steam: 'I'll publish my way out in five years!' "[5]

## Paying His Dues

Actually, twenty-three years passed before Fiedler made his per-manent departure from Montana. During that time, he published two seminal collections of essays, *An End to Innocence* (1955) and *No! In Thunder* (1960); a freshman reader, *The Art of the Essay* (1958); his first novel, *The Second Stone* (1963), and first collection of short stories, *Pull Down Vanity and Other Stories* (1962); a groundbreaking study of the American literary canon, *Love and Death in the American Novel* (1960); a more modest sequel to that work, *Waiting for the End* (1964); and scores of critical and creative efforts in some of the most distinguished literary journals in America. Nevertheless, he was known less for his productivity and insight than for his controversial personality. In 1963 Ronald Bryden wrote of him: "Shaking the dust of City College, so to speak, from his feet, he has lit out for the territory; and from the chair of English at Montana State University played the role of a prairie Tamburlaine, scourge of the East. . . . His stance . . . is that of the bawdy, bearded Western prophet, hurling contemptuous mischief at drawing-room 'culture,' little magazines and this week's good cause."[6]

Of course, Fiedler did not spend all of his time in Missoula, Montana. On several occasions during the fifties and sixties, he went east (once as far as the University of Athens) to teach on various fellowships. His earliest and most extended hegira occurred, however, when he served as a Japanese interpreter, interrogating prisoners of war for the U.S. Navy from 1942 to 1946 (followed by a year as a Rockefeller Fellow at Harvard from 1946 to 1947). This experience has given him a metaphor for his role as teacher and cultural commentator and has inspired a work-in-progress on Iwo Jima. And yet, he was uneasy serving as an authority figure. He remembers with chagrin an old Japanese lady asking him, "And how many women have you raped in the Great War?" over tea at the Detention Center in Saipan. But what really unnerved him most "was the prisoner about to be shaved of his pubic hair for hygienic reasons in a ship's sick bay off Iwo Jima, who, seeing my uniform over the doctor's shoulder, could only believe that the razor that fell toward his crotch threatened castration. And so he pissed all over himself in fright—afraid of *me!*" (*BB,* 41).

Back in Montana, Fiedler achieved a far more congenial degree of eminence when he was made a chief of the Blackfoot Indian tribe and renamed Heavy Runner. In this capacity, "he participated in various meetings on Indian affairs and the status of the Indians." "For two or three years," he told Patricia Ward Biederman, "I used to do the summary at the end of those. Indians love talking, you know, as I do. And instead of saying what people had actually said,

I would say what they had hoped to say or what they might have said, and they loved that." Fiedler goes on to note that his namesake was a famous chief of the Blackfeet (a mountain is named for him in Glacier National Park). "His family still lives. . . . We once went to an Indian dance in Missoula when my kids were little, and there was a girl called Eleanor Heavy Runner dancing, and the kids kept screaming, 'That's our cousin, that's our cousin!' "[7]

In the June 1948 *Partisan Review,* Fiedler published what is still his best-known and most controversial essay, "Come Back to the Raft Ag'in, Huck Honey!" In it he offers the novel thesis that the flight *from* civilization and "petticoat government" that dominates so many of our classic books is actually a flight *toward* the wilderness "antimarriage" of white and colored men. Had Fiedler used the discrete term *male bonding,* his essay would have been debated, but probably would not have caused such a furor. As it was, his several references to "homoerotic love" suggested that such novels as *Huckleberry Finn, Moby-Dick,* and the Leatherstocking Tales were actually X-rated fiction trying to pass as children's literature. Despite his misleading presentation, however, Fiedler's thesis has stood the test of time and is continually being vindicated by movies and television shows that pair a white hero and a dark-skinned sidekick. Indeed, one early review of the series *Star Trek* was entitled "Come Back to the Spaceship Ag'in, Spock Honey."

Fiedler's most ambitious, and to my mind most impressive, attempt to apply his pet theories to the entire pantheon of American literature came a dozen years later in his critical masterpiece, *Love and Death in the American Novel.* This was such an obviously major work that even those who had nothing good to say about it were forced to articulate their objections at great length. Significantly, these objections were hedged with enough begrudged praise to provide ample blurb material from even largely negative reviews. A perfect example is Richard Chase's long essay in the *Chicago Review,* "Leslie Fiedler and American Culture." Readers of the paperback edition of *Love and Death* are told (on the back cover) that Chase called this book "genuinely original . . . a work of lasting importance . . . a powerful indictment of our culture and modern culture in general." Turning to Chase's essay itself, however, we are not sure whether his comments, quoted out of context, were really meant as compliments. Chase excoriates Fiedler for bombast, sensationalism, factual inaccuracy, and a failure to acknowledge his indebtedness to other scholars. According to Chase, Fiedler is "a run-of-the-mill PhD candidate, a kind of archetype of the thousands who grimly and with what Fiedler calls a 'total moral commitment' nowadays study American literature and who submit articles to university quarterlies like *Modern Fiction Studies* entitled 'Theme and Structure in Absalom, Absalom!' or 'The Concept of Time in Sarah Orne Jewett.' " However, Fiedler's greatest sin in Chase's eyes is his profligate use of the exclamation mark: "He is the kind of author who can write: Herman Melville was born in New York in 1819!"[8]

In Missoula folks could not have cared less about Fiedler's eccentric views on American literature published in journals that many of them had never heard of. Their hackles were raised, however, by his reputation as a writer of "dirty" stories and poems. (One anonymous pamphleteer was moved to quote selected passages from Fiedler's fiction and verse: "pale flagrant breasts . . . thought seriously of making her . . . rested one hand gently on her ass . . . she wore nothing underneath, no girdle, no pants . . . a little tuft of hair where the buttocks . . . can't even remember to button our flies . . . nipples, not brownish or purple but really pink . . ." [see *BB*, 74]; all of which suggest something about the mentality of certain antipornographers.) The most notorious of the poems was a phallic hymn called "Dumb Dick." The most abused of the stories, a moving parable called "Nude Croquet," caused the issue of *Esquire* printing it to be banned in Knoxville, Tennessee. The fact that both works dealt with the decidedly antierotic theme of growing old carried no weight with Fiedler's local attackers. And when he defended himself in an essay entitled "On Becoming a Dirty Writer," those immune to irony took it as a confession of guilt.

Fiedler offended Montana chauvinists even further by publishing an excessively honest appraisal of his adopted home in *Partisan Review* under the title "Montana; or the End of Jean-Jacques Rousseau." Although he made several profound and subtle points in that essay, the passage that the locals focused on was his description of the "Montana face": "developed not for sociability or feeling, but for facing into the weather. It said friendly things to be sure, and meant them; but it had no adequate physical expressions even for friendliness, and the muscles around the mouth and eyes were obviously unprepared to cope with the demands of any more complicated emotion. . . . [T]he poverty of experience had left the possibilities of the human face in them incompletely realized" (*CE*, 1:135). It

was one thing to bring strange people into the state (as chairman
of the English Department, Fiedler had once hired a visiting poet
who, upon seeing a bevy of college girls in formals, "had cried aloud
among real estate agents and lawyers . . . —'My dears, I know
exactly how they feel. I used to be a mad queen myself' " [*BB*,
59]); it was quite another to hold the state up to the ridicule of
outsiders. Indeed, "the only unforgivable thing in the university or
the state was to be 'controversial' " (*BB*, 59).[9]

Whenever Fiedler found the world of the PTA and small-minded
civic boosterism to be too much for him, he would withdraw to the
seedy saloons which for him represented the real Montana. Entering
one such dive on a typical Saturday night, he notices "a 'Western
Combo,' complete with tenor, the guitars electrified and stepped
up so that 'Sixteen Tons' sounds like an artillery barrage and no one
is tempted to waste good drinking time by attempting conversation"
(*CE*, 2:335–36). On this particular occasion the young bartender,
a dropout from journalism school who is "only two years away from
the Near North Side of Chicago," is sporting a new pair of cowboy
boots:

"Worth thirty-five bucks," he says proudly, indicating the boots. "I got
'em from a wine-o just off the freights for half a gallon of muscatel. Christ,
he needed it bad. Walked next door to drink it (*we* don't let 'em drink
from bottles at the tables here, but next door they don't give a damn).
Walked out barefoot—*barefoot*—and it was snowing too. 'Take it or leave
it,' I told him, 'half a gallon for the boots.' They were red with yellow
threads but I had them dyed black. Look pretty good, don't they? Thirty-
five bucks." The band begins to play "You are my Sunshine," good and
loud and I can't hear any more, but I get it. I'm home. Montana or the
end of you know who. (*CE*, 2:336)

When he returned for a visit five years after leaving Missoula for
Buffalo, Fiedler noticed that a few familiar landmarks were gone:
"a new bridge replacing an old one from which a friend once nearly
jumped to her death; a new highway scarring the side of a hill where
my two oldest boys at five or six or seven used to play among
poisonous ticks for which we would search the hairline at the back
of their necks just before bedtime" (*CE*, 2:338). But the most
disconcerting change of all was the disappearance of two of his
favorite bars, one of which had been turned into a bohemian coffee
house. With fondness, he remembers "staggering out of its doors

one night, as blind drunk and happy as I have ever been in my life, my wife sagging on my arm, equally happy I hope (it was, I recall, a wedding anniversary); and there were a pair of cops waiting to greet us—and, in that lovely time before the fall of us all—to drive us home in jovial solicitude. 'Now take it easy, Doc, you're gonna be all right in the morning' " *(CE,* 2:340–41).

## Celebrity Nut

Leslie Fiedler is generally regarded as one of the most accomplished platform orators in academia. According to Benjamin DeMott:

> He rocks slightly as he speaks, his veins stand forth and his face sweats— a clever, bearded, tanned face, Mephistopheles one second, Santa Claus the next, the Saint Saens Samson after that. He seems almost to hum to himself, his rhythms and bits take on a Lenny Bruce beat, self-enjoyment sweeps up the room—good humor, vivacity. Even in his moments of scrinched-up, tortured, small-boy-cruelly-punished pain, the man's larger-than-life quality and relish of self are constant. Here before you, folks, here in this barrel torso sits the soul of the last appetitive, redskinned, thoroughly nonacademic academic on earth.[10]

In earlier times Fiedler probably would have been a featured performer on the Chautauqua circuit. But, because the Chautauqua is now dead, he must settle for a spot on the campus guest speakers' tour and on television talk shows. "There was a moment during the '60s," he tells us, "when the format of the *Merv Griffin Show,* for instance, had come to include—along with an aging actress, a current pop music star, and a stand-up comedian—a visiting 'nut,' at that point usually Allen Ginsberg or Norman Mailer, or occasionally, as it turned out, me" *(WWL,* 19).

Of course, Fiedler's status as a celebrity "nut" was due at least as much to the furor over his drug bust as to anything he had written. The media attention devoted to his case made him either a hero or a pariah to thousands who cared nothing for literary criticism but had definite opinions about the drug laws and the generation gap. Although Buffalo may not have been as provincial as Missoula, town-gown conflicts were exacerbated by the fact that what had once been a working-class, career-oriented community college (the University of Buffalo) was being transformed into a cosmopolitan liberal arts institution (the State University of New

York at Buffalo). Thus, many people in Fiedler's new hometown (especially alumni of the old University of Buffalo, such as assistant chief of detectives Michael Amico) were viscerally opposed to the bohemian values he represented. However, here (as elsewhere in America) tensions abated over the years, and Fiedler's dubious drug conviction was overturned in 1972.[11] Still, his life has been far from dull. Patricia Ward Biederman tells us that "In 1978, attired in pink tights and a smock, he was on location in Hollywood, making a 'Falstaffian' appearance in a low-budget, yet-to-be-released film based on a Grimm's fairy tale. He enjoyed leisurely lunches, good food and better talk with the late poet W. H. Auden on the island of Ischia. He has had his portrait sketched by director John Huston on a piece of cedar pulled from a cigar box. And he is virtually alone among critics in having had his name parodied by a ribald writer, Ray Kainen, who wrote one Dr. Lusty Fiddler into a book called *A Sea of Thighs*."[12]

During his first two decades at Buffalo Fiedler averaged a book a year, including a two-volume selection of his essays that ran to well over 1,000 pages; four more provocative critical studies: *The Return of the Vanishing American* (1968), *The Stranger in Shakespeare* (1972), *What Was Literature?: Class Culture and Mass Society* (1982), and *Olaf Stapledon: A Man Divided* (1983); four more volumes of fiction: *Back to China* (1965), *The Last Jew in America* (1966), *Nude Croquet and Other Stories* (1969), and *The Messengers Will Come No More* (1974); a partial autobiography—*Being Busted* (1970)—and a multidisciplinary meditation on human oddities called *Freaks: Myths and Images of the Secret Self* (1978). One of the results of his high visibility is that Fiedler has come to be regarded in certain circles as someone who "knows more things that aren't so than any man in America."[13]

This observation is cited as conventional wisdom in a generally snide essay by Grant Webster. What is most interesting about this essay is not that it is an attack on Fiedler (which has become something of a cottage industry in certain strata of academia), but that the main charge leveled against him is that he is a closet conservative. Rhetorical flamboyance, unconventional demeanor, and Marxist proclivities aside, Webster charges that Fiedler is obsessed "by a single theme: a rage at the loss of a patriarchal system of values and the consequent condemnation of modern American culture. . . . [H]e is outraged at the complexity of real adult life, where categories like

Mama and Papa are confused and he and everyone else are both male and female, active and passive, exploiter and exploited. . . . [A]fter two hundred years of the Romantic Revolution, only he remains to be shocked."[14]

Although Webster probably overstates his case, he has hit upon an aspect of Fiedler's thought that has eluded most other commentators—namely, that his war upon the status quo is often radical in the conservative, etymological sense of the term—he wishes to return to roots that far too many of his contemporaries have either repudiated or ignored altogether. A prime example is his adherence to ancient Jewish customs. In one of his more revealing essays ("Roman Holiday"), he tells of the extraordinary efforts he made to find a Passover seder one year in Rome. When he and his family finally succeeded in their quest, the service turned out to be "badly cut and extremely dull" (*CE*, 1:121). On their way home, they ran into an Italian Jewish couple who were excited not by the Passover, but by the success of a current transit strike: "This should be a lesson for De Gasperi and the Vatican, too," the husband said. When Fiedler mentioned that he was returning from a seder, the husband assumed he was joking. Upon discovering that he was not, the wife said: " 'How can you do it? . . . Do you mean to say that in this day and age you tell your children—' she could hardly manage to say it—'you teach them that we're the *Chosen People?*' " (*CE*, 1:123).

When Fiedler's first grandson was born, a decade and a half later, he decided that the infant should be circumcised "like all of his male ancestors for three thousand years" (*FR*, 382). Although a white-robed doctor from a nearby Protestant hospital was recruited to perform the surgical procedure, Fiedler himself presided over the religious ritual at a local commune in the presence of a congregation who, though mostly *goyim*, were "bearded and sandaled and robed quite like my own ultimate forebears." At the point in the ceremony "when the Celebrant says to the child, who actually bleeds in full view of all, his pain subdued by his first sip of wine, 'I say unto you, *In your blood live!*' Yea, I say unto you, *In your blood live!*' " the young man who stood behind Fiedler, "blond-bearded and blue eyed, his gentile head half a foot above my own, responded 'Heavy trip, man!' and fainted." "It was a response written in no prayerbook," Fiedler tells us, "but it was the right response. Because for once, for the first time in my fifty years of life, a *Birth,* a commemoration of our ancient Covenant with the God we thought dead was really *happening!*" (*FR*, 383).

Now in his late sixties, Fiedler is still scandalizing the academic elitists[15] (who panned *What Was Literature?*) and delighting his students at SUNY-Buffalo. Dropping in on a session of his under-graduate science fiction class in late 1983, David Gates observes: "It has been an hourlong improvisation—on such themes as 'E.T.,' Freud, Cabbage Patch dolls, the legends of Faust and Don Giovanni, Biblical prophecy, the history of feminism, Mary Shelley's 'Fran-kenstein,' the National Council of Churches' unisex lectionary, ABC-TV's 'The Day After'—which finally arrived at the ostensible topic, androgyny in the work of Ursula Le Guin, with five minutes left." "He has been doing these high-wire acts," Gates reminds us, "for the past four decades."[16]

What is in store for the decades to come is less certain. Although Fiedler has become disenchanted with writing criticism, he has several creative projects under way: his book on Iwo Jima, a spy novel partially set in the Bulgarian city of Varna (the port from which Dracula sailed), and the script for an episode of *Hill Street Blues*. At the same time, his life outside the classroom is less tur-bulent as he has finally come to be an accepted fixture in Buffalo. ("They know me," he says of the police. "They don't feel I'm a square anymore. There's a funny way in which cops distrust re-spectable citizens.")[17] Whether Fiedler has mellowed or the rest of the world has simply caught up with him is hard to say. It is perhaps significant, however, that the first chapter of *What Was Literature?* is entitled "Who Was Leslie A. Fiedler?"[18]

## Chapter Two
# The Word Made Flesh

As his critical stance has grown more aggressively anti-elitist, Fiedler has begun to feel profoundly uneasy about the scholarly attention devoted to his early theoretical essays. He would prefer to be known as the iconoclastic author of "Come Back to the Raft Ag'in, Huck Honey!" than as a pontifical Jungian. When he published *No! In Thunder* in 1960 he included "In the Beginning Was the Word: *Logos* or *Mythos*" and "Archetype and Signature: The Relationship of Poet and Poem," but felt compelled also to include the disclaimer that "they are examples of the kind of theorizing which threatens to leave literature and its appropriate delights for the sake of amateur philosophizing" (*CE*, 1:513). (By the time that he wrote *What Was Literature?* over two decades later, he was even claiming that these essays were academic put-ons.)[1] Nevertheless, these early manifestos help to define Fiedler's role in the backlash that was forming against the (no longer) new criticism in the 1950s.

Curiously enough, one of the main goals of the new criticism (hereafter referred to as formalism) was to free poetry from the confining notion that there was such a thing as inherently poetic subject matter. Formalists such as I. A. Richards and Cleanth Brooks argued for a poetry of inclusion, not of exclusion. With what Eliot called the "dissociation of sensibility," wit and intellect were purged from poetry—a development that led to an undue emphasis on inspiration and emotion in the romantic period as well as to the celebrated "high seriousness" of the Victorian Era.

By restoring irony, paradox, and extended metaphor to respectability (in short, by championing the metaphysical tradition in English poetry), the formalists succeeded in expanding the range of acceptable poetic content but in narrowing the range of acceptable poetic technique. In *Modern Poetry and the Tradition,* Brooks tends to underrate the verse of the eighteenth and nineteenth centuries. In *The Well Wrought Urn,* he tries (perhaps too ingeniously) to redeem the best of that verse by finding in it the qualities he most admires in the poetry of the seventeenth and twentieth centuries.

By virtually defining poetry in terms of its inclusiveness of texture and ambiguity, the formalists manage to exclude from the canon much literature that has moved people over the ages. Thus, Fiedler's more recent efforts to "open up the canon" may actually be prefigured in his early attacks on the righteous orthodoxies of formalism.

In emphasizing close reading of the text (what Fiedler and Douglas Bush dismiss as "remedial reading"), formalism helps us to see literature as an aesthetic mechanism. It shows us, in the words of John Ciardi, "how a poem means." As a result, it is less concerned with what literature is (or was) than with what specific texts ought to be. Fiedler's two seminal forays into theory, however, approach the task of criticism from the opposite perspective. Something of a mystic at heart, Fiedler sees the artist as neither copyist nor maker, but as priest—the shaman who sacramentalizes in song and story pure essences which (be they Platonic forms or Jungian archetypes) exist prior to experience.

One of the more intriguing features of Fiedler's "In the Beginning Was the Word" is its (perhaps unintended) affinity with the thought of formalist godfather John Crowe Ransom. In opposing logos and mythos to each other, Fiedler shares Ransom's belief that poetry and science constitute different modes of knowledge. Fiedler, however, defines the salient epistemological distinction as actually being between poetry and philosophy, "understanding philosophy in the older inclusive sense." Mythos, then, is the source of poetry, and logos the language of philosophy. Put another way: "philosophy invented *logos*, but *mythos* created poetry." Moreover, Fiedler observes, "poetry is historically the mediator between *logos* and *mythos*, the attempt to find a rationale of the pre-rational (which is to say, form)—and if philosophy quarrels with poetry, it is not because it considers its own mode of perception superior to the mythic way, but because it considers that there is *no* mode except its own; that mediation is therefore a betrayal of the truth" (*CE*, 1:518).

Where Fiedler parts company with Ransom and other formalists is in his metaphysics. Ransom values poetry over science because of its superior concreteness. Fiedler's preference for poetry, however, is due to its superior universality. It is the means by which we intuit "those archaic and persisting clusters of image and emotion which at once define and attempt to solve what is most permanent in the human predicament" (*CE*, 1:519). Whether we refer to these "archaic and persisting clusters" as archetypes, mythos, or simply myth, they are—in Fiedler's judgment—the very essence of poetry. This is because they are also the very essence of reality.

What poetry evokes in us that science cannot (and here Fiedler is once again close to Ransom) is a sense of reverence and astonishment—what earlier ages would have called the sublime. If we understand religion to involve dogma and institutionalized forms of worship, Fiedler is not making literature into religion. It would be more accurate to say that he regards man's natural piety toward the mythos as a necessary precondition for those human activities that we call religion and literature. Without that natural piety, "we can approach the given world only as an enemy or a bore" (*CE*, 1:521).

In attempting to place his critical insights within a metaphysical context, Fiedler is forced to make distinctions between the way things are and how they are understood (i.e., between ontology and epistemology). Borrowing Jacopo Mazzoni's notion that poetry is the "credible marvelous," he elaborates a series of conceptual categories: "The Marvelous as Marvelous is *mythos;* the Marvelous as Credible, Poetry; the Credible as Credible, philosophy and science; the Credible as Marvelous, the ersatz of Poetry which appears in ages oppressed by philosophy or science: rhetoric, journalism, *kitsch* . . ." (*CE*, 1:521). Thus conceived, the marvelous is not simply an adornment (or, worse yet, a distortion) of the rational, but a reality in its own right. Furthermore, if we regard Fiedler's series as an ontological hierarchy (a chain of being, if you will), then mythos is not only different from but superior to logos. As Fiedler once told a Communist guide in the Soviet Museum of Atheism, Michelangelo is closer to the truth than Darwin.

Fiedler's most famous theoretical essay, "Archetype and Signature," actually preceded his discourse on mythos and logos by six years, but it is printed after the later piece in both *No! In Thunder* and *Collected Essays.* This revised order makes thematic sense in that the distinction between mythos and logos posits the ontological roots of poetry, while the interaction of archetype and signature accounts for the existence of actual poems. (It may be that Fiedler felt a need to write his second essay as an elucidating context for his first.)

"Archetype and Signature" begins with a ringing polemical indictment of the formalist dogma that criticism ought not to concern itself with the lives of poets, but only with their works. Although he is shrewd enough to focus on the more laughable excesses of the more simple-minded formalists (e.g., publishing anthologies in which the poems are printed out of chronological order and without the names of the authors attached), Fiedler is not simply setting up a straw man. What he finds distressing about the formalist critics is not that they occasionally descend into self-parody (a hazard from which Fiedler himself has not always been immune), but that their understanding of art is essentially nominalist. Such a position, Fiedler argues, is "metaphysically reprehensible" (*CE,* 1:529).

Nominalism, we will recall, is one of the traditional responses to the epistemological dilemma of the one and the many. Simply put, nominalism holds that only individual entities exist. Universal concepts are nothing more than names that we devise for groups of objects. Hence, we have classroom texts such as Thomas and Brown's *Reading Poems,* the very title of which "reveals the dogma . . . [that] in a world of discrete, individual 'experiences,' of 'close reading' (a cant phrase of the antibiographist) as an ideal, one cannot even talk of so large an abstraction as poetry" (*CE,* 1:534). In contrast, Fiedler's Neoplatonic leanings (known in the jargon of philosophy as "conceptual realism") make it not only possible but necessary to talk about abstractions; for in this philosophical tradition, particular entities are the incarnation of universal concepts.

In leveling his criticisms at the "anti-biographists," Fiedler is gracious (or devious) enough to make some strategically insignificant concessions. He admits, for example, that a poem cannot be regarded as the sum total of its author's intentions. What the formalists have done is to distort that valid insight into the rather extravagant contention "that nothing the poet can tell us about his own work is of any *decisive* importance" (*CE,* 1:533).

Responding to this claim, Fiedler declares that "the notion of 'intention' implies the belief that there is a somehow existent something against which the achieved work of art can be measured; and although this has been for all recorded time the point of view of the practicing writer, every graduate student who has read Wimsatt and Beardsley's ponderous tract on the Intentional Fallacy knows that we are all now to believe that there is no poem except the poem of 'words' " (*CE,* 1:533). And yet, to see that a knowledge of intention is essential to understanding the aesthetic meaning of an act, we need only remember why we laugh at "the visiting dignitary in the high hat when he slips on the steps to the platform"

(*CE*, 1:533). By the same token, we must speak of what a poem obviously aims at to judge what it actually achieves.

Like early Christian heretics, the formalists are dangerous not because they are totally wrong (for then they could be dismissed as harmless cranks), but because they are partially right. The genteel formulation is to say that they have provided a needed corrective to past excesses. In Fiedler's judgment, those excesses include two egregious misuses of biography by supposed literary critics: the extreme subjectivism of latter-day romantics and the arid pedantry of what Gore Vidal calls scholar-squirrels (of the latter Fiedler writes: "so long as notes proving that Milton was born in one house rather than another continue to be printed in magazines devoted to the study of literature, people will be tempted into opposite though equal idiocies, which have at least not been for so long proved utterly bankrupt" [*CE*, 1:534]). In an attempt to "redeem" poetry from the nominalism of the close reader and the "opposite though equal idiocies" of the romantic and the pedant, Fiedler asks that we think of the poem as "Archetype" and "Signature."

Fiedler is not using the word "Archetype" in a narrow Jungian sense (what he speaks of may reside in the Jungian Collective Unconscious or in the Platonic world of Ideas). Instead, he means what in his later essay he will call mythos: "the immemorial patterns of response to the human situation in its most permanent aspects: death, love, the biological family, the relationship with the Unknown, etc." By "Signature," Fiedler means "the sum total of individuating factors in a work, the sign of the Persona or Personality through which an Archetype is rendered, and which itself tends to become a subject as well as a means of the poem." Consequently, literature "can be said to come into existence at the moment a Signature is imposed upon the Archetype" (*CE*, 1:537). Because of their nominalist predilections, formalists would disavow the archetype; because of their antibiographical prejudices, they would disregard the signature.

And yet, as Fiedler amply demonstrates, the formalist critic is sometimes forced to violate in practice what he asserts in theory. By expressing a willingness to study an author's "idiosyncratic use of words," even the most adamant antibiographist admits that information outside the text of the poem can sometimes be necessary to an understanding of the poem. If that is so, Fiedler asserts, then such information must also be useful for purposes of evaluation. If we have poems printed without the poet's name, as is done in the Thomas and Brown text, how can we even recognize the tendency of William Shakespeare and John Donne to pun on their own names? Without that knowledge, we are prevented from evaluating the aesthetic function of the pun within the poem.

Because Fiedler does not share the formalist's obsession for staying inside the poem, his critical stance is enriched by an openness to history (including the personal history of the poet's own life). However, because archetypes are not bound by time, he is also freed from the temporal parochialism of the traditional scholar-squirrel; he speaks not of "influences," but of "confluences." Whereas conventional academic hacks would reject a Freudian reading of Shakespeare on the grounds that Shakespeare preceded Freud, Fiedler would say that the poet has simply intuited that which the psychoanalyst would later explicate. The (biographical) fact that Freud drew much of his imagery and vocabulary from literature would tend to strengthen the notion that he was simply putting his personal signature on immortal archetypes.

Fiedler concludes his essay with a discussion of the archetype that makes all of literature possible—that of the poet. In an age when myth is first becoming literature (i.e., when the archetype is "reaching tentatively toward a Signature"), the poet is regarded as a passive conduit through which the Muse speaks. When the communal system of belief breaks down, the poet is perceived as more signature than archetype (the alienated egoist) and is consequently stigmatized by society. We currently live in such a fragmented age, deprived of "Greek myths, the fairy tales and *novelle* of the Elizabethans, the Christian body of legend available to Dante" (*CE,* 1:545).[2]

We can discern at least three separate strategies that contemporary writers have devised for confronting this dilemma. Artists such as Graham Greene and Robert Penn Warren have sought to elevate the forms of "popular art" (where a formulaic body of narratives still exists) to the level of high literature. Poets can also "ironically manipulate the shreds and patches of outlived mythologies" (*CE,* 1:546); this has essentially been the approach of T. S. Eliot, James Joyce, Ezra Pound, and Thomas Mann. Then, there is the extreme expedient—employed by William Blake, W. B. Yeats, and Hart Crane—of devising one's own private myth system.

Rejecting all three of these approaches, Fiedler suggests that in our atomized culture the poet cannot redeem, create, or reconstitute a common body of stories; but is left instead only with himself as archetype—with the archetype of the poet. By plumbing the depths of his own psyche, he can transcend the eccentricities of signature and return "to his unconscious core, where he becomes one with us all in the presence of our ancient Gods, the protagonists of fables we think we no longer believe. . . . It is a process to delight a Hegelian, the triple swing from a naive communal to a personal to a sophisticated communal" (*CE,* 1:547).

Because "Archetype and Signature" is such an obviously polemical attack on the accepted dogmas of formalism (and published in the *Sewanee Review,* no less), it was inevitable that the endangered orthodoxy would fight back. Unfortunately, the most famous rebuttal to Fiedler's irreverent essay (a page and a half in Wimsatt and Brooks's *Literary Criticism: A Short History*) is little more than a supercilious misreading of some serious—if outrageous—ideas. This misreading is abetted by Fiedler's tendency to make flashy generalizations which, when read out of context (and sometimes even in context), strike the more sober among us as preposterous. Thus, Wimsatt and Brooks gleefully pounce on the statement that "in our day, it is even possible to be a writer without having written anything!"[3] Although Fiedler is not really concerned with such a poet-manqué (and mentions him only in passing), Wimsatt and Brooks seem to suggest that it is far saner to think of a poem as only words than to disregard words altogether.

The most damaging charge leveled against Fiedler is that he regards a poem not as "an object to be known, . . . [but as] a clue to an event in the poet's psyche."[4] This is, of course, nonsense. Fiedler most assuredly does regard the poem as "an object to be known"; however, unlike Wimsatt and Brooks, he believes that a familiarity with the poet's life can aid in the act of knowing.[5] Biography is thus a means to an end, not an end in itself. Moreover, to argue that "the archetypal materials are really a privileged poetic subject matter in disguise"[6] is to make the fantastic claim that Fiedler wants to narrow the literary canon. Actually, his concept of mythos (or archetypes) simply identifies the origins of literature, and does so in a way broad enough to include far more than Wimsatt and Brooks are likely to admit to the canon.

What comes next is a shoddy example of selective quotation, beginning with Fiedler's statement: "In the Mask of his life and the manifold masks of his work, the poet expresses for a whole society the ritual meaning of its inarticulate selves; the artist goes forth not to 'recreate the conscience of his race,' but to redeem its unconscious. We cannot get back into the primal Garden of the unfallen Arche-types, but we can yield ourselves to the dreams and images that mean paradise regained."[7] Wimsatt and Brooks then cite Fiedler's earlier observation that what resides at the core of the unconscious are "fables we think we no longer believe." These two erstwhile foes of the intentional fallacy then feign confusion about how one can unconsciously believe things that he thinks he no longer believes (as if they had never heard the aphorism about there being no atheists in a foxhole).

The impression that is left is that Fiedler not only does not know what he is talking about, but that he does not care to know. Within Fiedler's scheme, however, the artist, not the critic, is an uncon-scious seer. The paragraph that Wimsatt and Brooks have quoted only in part goes on to say: "For the critic, who cannot only yield but must also *understand,* there are available new methods of ex-ploration. To understand the Archetypes of Athenian drama, he needs (above and beyond semantics) anthropology; to understand those of recent poetry, he needs (beyond 'close analysis') depth anal-ysis, as defined by Freud and, particularly, by Jung" (*CE,* 1:547).

The joint effort with Wimsatt represented at least the second attempt Cleanth Brooks had made to respond to "Archetype and Signature." The first appeared in the *Sewanee Review* shortly after the publication of Fiedler's essay. Entitled "A Note on the Limits of 'History' and the Limits of 'Criticism,' " this defense of formal-ism is actually the last installment in a running debate between Brooks and Douglas Bush over the meaning of Marvell's "Horatian Ode." Brooks had originally published a close reading of Marvell's poem in the 1946 *English Institute Essays,* only to find that reading challenged by Bush on historical grounds in the summer 1952 issue of the *Sewanee Review* (Fiedler's essay had appeared in the spring issue). While defending himself against the attack of the traditional scholar, Brooks felt compelled to add a few words about Fiedler's more general assault on formalist orthodoxy, his strategy being to depict Bush and Fiedler as opposite sides of the same coin.

Although he admits that Bush and Fiedler would find each other to be strange bedfellows, Brooks notes that both are attempting to restore biographical and historical considerations to the analysis of literature. Summarizing Fiedler's "neat, almost jaunty survey of recent literary history," Brooks writes: "If I may fill in some names, Mr. Fiedler might presumably see Mr. Bush as the thesis (the old fashioned historical scholarship), me as the antithesis (the doctrinaire antibiographer), and himself as the triumphant synthesis."[8] There are, however, other ways of looking at the situation. Eschewing dialectics for dichotomy, Brooks sees formalism as the only pure criticism and all other approaches as hybrids of nonliterary disciplines (religion, sociology, anthropology, and the like).

"In their concern for the break-up of the modern world," Brooks writes, "Mr. Bush, Mr. Fiedler, and a host of other scholars and critics are anxious to see literature put to work to save the situation."[9] Although Brooks professes to share his adversaries' desire to redeem our disintegrating, deracinated culture, he thinks it dangerous to confuse religion and poetry. Such confusion ultimately serves neither God nor art: "though poetry has a very important role in any culture, to ask that poetry save us is to impose a burden on poetry that it cannot sustain. The danger is that we shall merely get an ersatz religion and an ersatz poetry."[10]

The distinction that Brooks makes between his position and Fiedler's is judicious, and his arguments quite tenable. He is positing the conventional Judeo-Christian separation of the sacred from the profane. Fiedler, however, subscribes to the mystical tradition that sees religion not as a specific category of experience, but as the underlying reality of all experience. Although Fiedler speaks of mythos and archetypes (terms which do not carry the sectarian baggage of "religion"), he is clearly dealing with what he regards as spiritual and metaphysical realities. As an orthodox Christian, Brooks believes in a religion of incarnation. As a myth guru, Fiedler believes in a literature of incarnation. For him, the words of a poem are never merely words, but some primordial Word made flesh.

*Chapter Three*

# Typologies

To be called everything from seminal to sophomoric is the predictable fate of a critic as bold and flamboyant as Leslie Fiedler. Whether he is regarded as a startlingly original thinker or as a thesis-ridden poseur, Fiedler commands attention for the novelty of his insights. One tendency that runs through much of his writing is the impulse to categorize literary traditions and paradigms of experience (the concepts of archetype and signature, and logos and mythos are cases in point). This impulse is no doubt due to Fiedler's epistemological preference for (conceptual) realism over nominalism. Even when the categories he discusses are original with him, Fiedler speaks more with the wonder of discovery than with the pride of invention.

## Dionysus and the Privy

In reflecting on his career in *What Was Literature?*, Fiedler asks us to believe that his most ostensibly serious writings ("Archetype and Signature" and "In the Beginning Was the Word") were actually intended to be parodies of academic pretentiousness, while his more outrageous work (e.g., "Come Back to the Raft Ag'in, Huck Honey!") is his most truly serious. If this is so, one hardly knows how to approach such an exasperating and eclectic essay as *"Chutzpah* and *Pudeur."* However, one might begin by placing it in the context of its author's career. Originally written in 1969, *"Chutzpah* and *Pudeur"* concludes Fiedler's 1971 sequence of essays *Cross the Border—Close the Gap*. ("In the Beginning Was the Word" and "Archetype and Signature" occupy a similarly climactic position in the 1960 collection *No! In Thunder*.) Thus, shunning the strictures of the doctrinaire antibiographer, we might regard *"Chutzpah* and *Pudeur"* as an index of how far Fiedler's theoretical sensibility had developed over the watershed decade of the sixties.

By his third paragraph Fiedler acknowledges the tradition in which he is working. Viewing literature in terms of a neat dichotomy is an ancient critical pastime, two of the more recent examples of which are Matthew Arnold's concept of Hebraic and Hellenic and Philip Rahv's more parochial denomination of Redskin and Paleface. Fiedler's effort is distinguished from those of Arnold and Rahv because he sees his polar terms as referring not to two discrete categories of literature (or writers), but to two complementary aspects of the creative process. His approach here tends to be more Freudian than Jungian; but in its mixture of high and low rhetoric, scholarly erudition and vernacular crudity—indeed of *pudeur* and *chutzpah*—this essay is most unmistakably Fiedlerian.

*Pudeur* is, of course, a French term that refers to a sense of modesty and tact, particularly in sexual matters. Psychologically, *pudeur* seems most appropriately connected with anality. Early toilet training teaches one the propriety of excreting in private. By the same token, writing is for many artists much of the time (and probably for all some of the time) primarily an act of concealment. It may be an assertion of the ego, but it is one that is done in terms of conventions (some inherited, some improvised) that conceal the personality of the author. Because the mask of traditional literary forms (pastoral elegy and the like)[1] is largely inaccessible to modern writers, we find such contrived diversions as "the reticence of Emily Dickinson, the endless qualifications of Henry James, the playful assault on syntax and punctuation of e. e. cummings" (*CE,* 2:519).

Against the decorous French term Fiedler opposes the vulgar Yiddish one. *Chutzpah* could well be defined as a brazen lack of modesty, an urge to exhibit rather than to conceal the self. If literature arises generically from the interaction of archetype and signature, it emerges psychologically from the dialectical clash of *chutzpah* and *pudeur*. Indeed, Fiedler's more recent pair of terms is not totally unrelated to his earlier one. To talk about archetypes as the stuff of our collective unconscious serves the *pudique* function of hiding the individuating aspects of the poet's personality. At the same time, the artist's signature can be seen as a product of his *chutzpah*. Although one characteristic or the other may seem dominant in particular writers or even in particular ages, the tension between *chutzpah* and *pudeur* is always present and "plays a large part in determining our essential double view of what it is the artist says or does or makes" (*CE,* 2:517).

Because writing is a verbal act, Fiedler is tempted to equate *chutzpah* with orality, thus connecting the "artist's two conflicting

impulses . . . with the mythological orifices on either end of the
alimentary canal" (*CE*, 2:520). As we know from experience, the
person with *chutzpah* tends to run off at the mouth. But, even more
fundamentally, *chutzpah* is what is commonly known as "balls."
Thus, Fiedler hits upon an even more suggestive equation for the
procreative side of his polarity. "Like onanism," he writes, "the
creation of 'literature' is an auto-erotic act, accompanied by, or rather
creating, maintaining, certain fantasies. But in the realm of 'literature' the auto-erotic act itself remains invisible, existing only in
metaphor, by analogy; while the fantasies, once they have been
committed to writing, are quite visible, palpable, one is tempted
to say, real. But this is, of course, quite the opposite of masturbation" (*CE*, 2:524).

The two literary forms that best exemplify the dialectic between
*chutzpah* and *pudeur* are the pornographic poem and that enigmatic
figure that has been called everything from a riddle to a (metaphysical) conceit. On the one hand, we have the arrogant, *chutzpahdik* poet (e.g., Walt Whitman or Allen Ginsberg), who "must first
be condemned as 'the dirtiest beast of the age,' then, not cleared
of that charge but found through it, loved for it." On the other
hand, "the shamefast poet . . . must first be blamed for his *obscurity,*
then without being absolved, found through it and loved for it,
quite like Gerard Manley Hopkins." Fiedler continues this unlikely
pairing of Whitman and Hopkins (*chutzpah* and *pudeur*) by reminding us of Hopkins's surprising declaration of his spiritual affinity
with Whitman: "It is as close to confessing the particular guilt that
dogged him, the homosexuality he shared with Whitman, as Hopkins could come; but it is also a reminder of the sense in which
*chutzpah* and *pudeur* are originally and finally one, two faces of a
single ambivalence" (*CE*, 2:533).

The problems with this analysis are obvious. If Hopkins is really
making a veiled allusion to that *pudique* term *sexual preference,* then
the dialectic between *chutzpah* and *pudeur* is reduced to that between
"flaming fag" and "closet queen"; which, in any event, seems a
limited way of looking at poets as rich and complex as Whitman
and Hopkins. If, however, we regard the dissociation of sensibility
as the separation of *chutzpah* and *pudeur,* then we might profitably
look at the (pre-dissociation) poetry of seventeenth-century England to find a fruitful coupling of the two paradigm impulses of
the literary artist. As a vehicle for erotic thought (which is figur-

atively, and sometimes even literally, the ultimate in *felt* thought), the enigma, riddle, or extended simile employs *pudeur* in the service of *chutzpah*. When erotic and violent conceits are used as a means of poetically sacramentalizing the holy (as in, for example, John Donne's "Batter my heart, three person'd God"), the process becomes fully dialectical: *chutzpah* and *pudeur* are joined to redeem a vision of their prefallen synthesis; for it was only after committing the ultimate *chutzpah* in Eden that man required the *pudeur* of the fig leaf. But I digress.

As Fiedler notes, the fall that had the more far-reaching implications for literature was not the one in Eden but the one at Babel. Here, at the site of "their presumably unlimited erection," built with their own hands, men experienced a fall not "from grace into morality," but "from the Tongue into many tongues, from 'Revelation' to 'literature' " (*CE,* 2:521), perhaps even from archetype to signature. In a sense, *chutzpah* and *pudeur* are simply different responses to the fall at Babel. The swagger of the poet who dares to say "I" and to say it in the vernacular is a profane celebration of the fall to literature. Over against this act of celebration is a tradition of shame that believes that, if only the vernacular can be suppressed, we can find our way back to unity. The ordaining of Latin as the Holy Tongue of the Catholic Mass was an attempt to reverse Babel, an act of ecclesiastical *pudeur.* In the humanistic religion of high culture, the attempt to make a literary canon of books written in an elevated form of the vernacular is a similarly wishful act of historical regression.

Reflecting on the current situation, Fiedler writes: "Without an adequate faith to justify it, any venture at defining a canonical literature, like any attempt to separate a sacred language from a profane, is revealed as one more spasm prompted by the castrating shame which has been haunting Western Art ever since the first Western artist set out to sing of sex and the 'I.' The chill that freezes the marrow of worshippers at the altars of High Art is not just the cold that possesses all empty churches, but the zero weather of the Eternal Winter, which sets a new generation of readers to shivering even in our superheated classrooms and libraries" (*CE,* 2:539). With this passage, the terms of the dichotomy have shifted from *chutzpah* and *pudeur* to Dionysus and Apollo.

It would be nice to believe, with Levi-Straus, that one can reject the extremes of Eternal Summer and Eternal Winter (Dionysus and

Apollo) for the balanced periodicity of the seasons (the fully integrated personality). Fiedler argues, however, that we have lost the
rhythm of the seasons "in a world of air-conditioning and travel so
rapid that summer and winter are hours rather than months apart"
(CE, 2:540). Moreover, it is only in art, never in nature, that perfect
harmony and equilibrium are achieved. Thus, if one must choose
between extremes, Fiedler will opt for the *chutzpah* of Dionysus over
the *pudeur* of Apollo. Like the Bacchae themselves, he sees in the
orgy a utopian image of community.

At a considerably less theoretical level, Fiedler explores what
might be a variation of the *chutzpah/pudeur* dialectic in "Caliban or
Hamlet: A Study in Literary Anthropology." As his old *Partisan
Review* editor Philip Rahv had done in "Paleface and Redskin,"
Fiedler attempts to divide classic American writers into highbrow
(Apollonian, *pudique*) and lowbrow (Dionysian, *chutzpahdik*) categories. He goes beyond Rahv, however, in relating this distinction
to the images that Europeans harbor of Americans and that Americans harbor of themselves. Because these images are rooted in literature but have extraliterary ramifications, Fiedler invents the hybrid
discipline of literary anthropology. Within the context of this discipline, Americans have alternately been viewed as Caliban or Hamlet.

For nearly 300 years before the "United States" came into being,
"America" was a realm accessible to the European imagination.
During this time, one of the most mythically potent attempts to
visualize the "brave new world" across the sea was *The Tempest,* a
play that Leo Marx has called "Shakespeare's American Fable."[2] Even
today, many Europeans share Shakespeare's vision of the indigenous
American as Caliban, *"l'homme sauvage* of an already existing mythology transplanted to the New World: part Indian, part Negro,
all subhuman" (CE, 2:293). Thus, when Americans—particularly
American writers—are most primitive, nativist, and provincial,
they are closest to emulating the European stereotype of them. (This
may go a long way toward explaining European enthusiasm for such
examples of American popular culture as country music, hardboiled
detective novels, and Jerry Lewis.) It is no accident that Swift's
persona gives an American credit for his "modest proposal."

When John F. Kennedy was assassinated, Europeans (and many
Americans) found it easier to attribute the act to a brutish Caliban
than to "a lonely and isolated individual who is diseased or deranged

in mind" (see *CE,* 2:286). And yet, in declaring Lee Harvey Oswald to have been the lone assassin, the Warren Commission opted for the latter paradigm—for Hamlet over Caliban. Paradoxically, Americans are most themselves not when they are attempting to live up to an image that Europeans created for them even before they existed as a people, but rather when they "permit themselves . . . freely to ransack their whole cultural heritage (Hebraic-Hellenistic-Renaissance-Romantic, all that they share with Europe); and when they end choosing . . . at first hand whatever they will" (*CE,* 2:289). When this has happened, Fiedler maintains, the image of Hamlet has been most often chosen.

This Hamlet analogy, like that of Caliban, is influenced by our relationship to Europe. It enables us to play, however, not the rebellious slave, but the wronged son. I suspect that insofar as we think of ourselves only in the context of America, the Adamic prototype is our most compelling self-image. But when we feel the tug of the umbilical cord that ties us to our Old World mother, we become that second Adam, Christ or even that second Christ, Hamlet: "For archetypally speaking, Hamlet is Christ after the death of God" (*CE,* 2:292). America's compulsion to save the rest of the world (at least the Western or European world) from whatever particular monster happens to be at the gate is the impulse of a dutiful son. (Carrying this conceit a step farther, one might wonder whether excessive self-doubt will ultimately render the American Hamlet impotent before the Soviet Fortinbras.)

At the time that Fiedler was writing (1965), the Dionysian-Redskin-Caliban image was in vogue. Whitman seemed a more vital figure than Eliot; the Beats and their various spin-offs were still an important cultural influence; and even such elegant stylists as Norman Mailer and James Baldwin were remaking themselves as holy barbarians. (Although Fiedler mentions only Karl Shapiro, the same transformation was taking place in American poetry, as early formalists such as Robert Lowell and Robert Penn Warren were experimenting with more open and confessional verse.) In the two decades since then, the introspective, self-referential Hamlets of postmodernism have come to dominate high, canonical literature, with popular culture increasingly becoming the domain of Caliban. Predictably, Fiedler has chosen to follow the living beast rather than the dying prince.

## On the Good Ship Lollipop

A more universal cultural prototype than either Caliban or Hamlet
is the child as moral paradigm. Although Christ may have said that
a little child will lead them, the notion that "innocence" is a goal
for which all men should strive is largely a product of the psychic
revolution known as romanticism and, indeed, helps to define that
revolution. In addressing this phenomenon in "The Eye of Innocence" ("some notes on the role of the child in literature"), Fiedler
once again ventures into literary anthropology.

The cult of the child was not possible as long as Western Christianity held to an absolute interpretation of Original Sin. "If one
began by believing that an originally corrupted nature must be
trained (cajoled and beaten) into the semblance of orderly virtue,
he ended by being convinced that an adult had some chance of
attaining goodness, the child little or none" (CE, 1:473). Romanticism not only rejected this traditional doctrine, but stood it on
its head. Original Innocence now replaced Original Sin, and the
process of maturation was regarded not as a climb toward Heaven,
but as a fall from primordial goodness. In an age when the greatest
compliment one could pay to an author was to say that he was
secretly of the Devil's party, the child became not a candidate for
damnation, but—as Wordsworth would have it—"father of the
Man."

The emergence of child worship at the same time that Europe
was discovering for the imagination the New World that had earlier
been discovered for the geographers made the child part of a sentimental primitivism that was virtually to define the American
experience. (As difficult as it may have been for some to imagine a
return to the historic Eden, all can envision a regression to childhood.) Moreover, the child is the "one safely genteel symbol of
protest" against bourgeois culture. For the romantic to glorify "the
peasant . . . over the city dweller; the idiot or the buffoon over
the philosopher; woman over man—and within the female sex, the
whore over the bourgeoisie" (CE, 1:476), was to threaten middle-
class values in a disturbingly obvious way. However, to love children, no matter how subversive the motivation, was simply to join
ranks with decent people everywhere.

To the Anglo-Saxon mind, the supreme embodiment of childhood
innocence is "the Good Good Girl, the blonde asexual goddess of

nursery or orphanage, reincarnated from Little Nell to Mary Pick-
ford" (*CE*, 1:477). In this figure the worship of the female is combined with an idealization of virginity. Thus, the Divine Boy of
orthodox Christianity has been replaced by a female counterpart
"imagined not in the arms of the mother but in those of the father,
and not at the moment of birth but at that of death." What Fiedler
is referring to here is the Protestant Pietà: "the white-clad daughter,
dying or dead, in the arms of the Old Man, tearful papa or grandfather or woolly-haired slave" (*CE*, 1:478). In this shamelessly sentimental scene we can indulge our prurient desire to violate, indeed
destroy, an unbearable symbol of innocence. Also, in a culture where
the Good Good Girl is deprived of the refuge of the nunnery, it is
only in death that her purity (and her maidenhead) can remain intact.

Although the Good Good Girl is a staple of both the British and
the American imagination, the Good Good Boy remains an essentially Old World figure, "the juvenile reminder of a tradition of
aristocratic culture" which Americans have left behind (*CE*, 1:481).
Consequently, American literature offers us no counterpart to Tiny
Tim, Paul Dombey, or Oliver Twist (much less Little Lord Faun-
tleroy). Even as a pauper, the Good Good Boy strikes Americans
as effete and priggish. When such a figure does appear in our
literature (from Twain's Sid Sawyer to *MASH*'s Charles Emerson
Winchester III), it is as an object of derision, a comic foil to the
true American hero—the Good Bad Boy (from Tom Sawyer to
Hawkeye Pierce).

The Good Bad Boy is the mischievous scamp who violates adult
notions of propriety without ever doing anything seriously wrong
(e.g., Dennis the Menace sitting in the corner with his teddy bear
at his side). Although the sissy is often called a "mama's boy,"
Fiedler argues that all American boys belong to mother. The difference between him and the scamp is that "the Good Good Boy
does what his mother must pretend to the rest of the world (even
to herself) that she wants him to do, obey, conform; the Good Bad
Boy does what she *really* wants him to do: deceive, break her heart
a little, so that she can forgive him, smother him in the embrace
that seals him back into her world forever" (*CE*, 1:481). Had the
Parable of the Prodigal Son been set in America, the forgiving parent
undoubtedly would have been female.

According to the sentimental view of childhood, the one characteristic shared by both the Good Good Girl and the Good Bad

Boy is the lack of sexual imagination. If evil is to be equated with the id and the child to remain a symbol of purity, then even the most innocent forms of genital curiosity must be denied to those prepubescent icons. Other representations of the primitive or instinctual life could be divided into benign and demonic opposites: "Woman becomes the Fair Virgin and the Dark Lady, the Indian becomes Mingo and Mohawk, Pawnee and Sioux—Good Indian and Bad Indian!" (*CE,* 1:486). But the child, whose imaginative reality is explicitly defined by his (and particularly her) innocence, resists such bifurcation. Thus childhood sexuality is dealt with obliquely or, more often, ignored altogether.

As Fiedler notes, however, Mark Twain came perilously close to blowing the cover from this subterfuge when, in that famous scene from Tom Sawyer, Becky is almost caught looking at nude pictures in the teacher's anatomy book. When Tom surprises her, she accidentally tears one of the pictures; and he, in a gesture of gallantry worthy of Sidney Carton, confesses to her crime and suffers her punishment. Fortunately for the myth of the child, we remember Tom's gallantry, not the act of voyeurism that inspired it. "[I]t is as necessary for him," Fiedler writes, "that Becky retain her mythical Goodness as it is for her that he retain his equally legendary Badness. It is hard to know which revelation would seem more scandalous: that she is not as pure as she is postulated, or that he is not as wicked" (*CE,* 1:488). [3]

By the time we reach the mid-twentieth century, things have changed considerably. Whereas Twain was "squeamish about sex, [but] utterly frank about violence" (*CE,* 1:489), today's sentimentalists have reversed the equation. The sexual revolution has liberated the id from the superego, and material affluence has created a postpubescent extension of childhood known as adolescence: "The Good Bad Boy can get himself laid these days even in the fiction of Anglo-Saxondom, but he is no longer permitted to glory in beating up on the Jewish kid next door, or the minister's son or the overdressed stranger from the big city" (*CE,* 1:491). It is not surprising that at the time Fiedler was writing many of our more popular novelists were themselves overgrown adolescents—Good Bad Boys such as J. D. Salinger, laureate of prep-school angst, and Jack Kerouac, bohemian Huck Finn (or perhaps only Tom Sawyer) dreaming that he was Nigger Jim.

If the adolescent has replaced the child as moral exemplar in much contemporary literature, our vision has not necessarily become more sophisticated. (Huck Finn and numerous other nineteenth-century "children" were chronologically adolescents, but—because the category had not yet been invented—were never regarded as such.) We may simply have created another noble savage to serve as an indictment of civilization (here identified with the maturity of adult life). The James Dean prototype is a rebel without a cause not because his rebellion is gratuitous, but because his cause is too obvious to require a name. It is no longer the Good Good Girl who redeems us for bourgeois respectability, but the Good Bad Boy who leads us to existential authenticity.

As an outcast from society, the Good Bad Boy forms alliances with adults who are also outcast. Indeed, he may even learn the sacramental forms of rebellion (drink, indolence, and the like) from his adult mentor. The bonding of the child and the bum (as in William Faulkner's "Uncle Willy" and *The Reivers*) has become a commonplace in both our national literature and our national life. As Fiedler suggests, the figure of Rip Van Winkle may well be "the Good Bad Boy grown old without growing up" (*CE,* 1:497). Unlike Peter Pan, who managed to remain a child in Never-Never Land, Rip negotiates a passage from first to second childhood by sleeping through his adult years.[4] Such a passage is even easier for the Negro or Indian, because the Dame Van Winkles (and Miss Watsons) of this world have never considered the savage as more than a child (and sometimes as a good deal less).

For purposes of dramaturgy, the innocence of the child must be portrayed against a background of adult corruption. This results in a curious variation on the age-old theme of initiation. Traditionally, the rite of passage leads the child into adulthood and, thus, involves a loss of innocence. To an orthodox Christian or classical sensibility such a process, though often painful, is both necessary and desirable. Theologically, this is the notion of the fortunate fall, the psychological equivalent of which is the basis for much of the tragic irony at the heart of canonical American literature. For the sentimentalist, however, innocence remains the supreme value. What is needed, then, is a form of initiation that introduces the child to the evil of the adult world without making him a part of it. Here, the child "is not a participant in the fall, but a *witness,* only vicariously inducted into the knowledge of sin" (*CE,* 1:500).

The Child as Peeping Tom has become a familiar presence in
modern literature. In works as diverse as Henry James's *What Maisie
Knew,* Sherwood Anderson's "I Want to Know Why," Thomas
Berger's *Little Big Man,* and even James Joyce's "Araby," children
lose some of their illusions as a result of chance encounters with
adult sexuality. The child thus acquires a knowledge of evil, while
maintaining his own innocence. Even when he is tempted by the
flesh, he is protected as if by a guardian angel. Robin's refusal to
follow the girl in scarlet petticoats in Hawthorne's "My Kinsman,
Major Molineux" may be attributed to his Puritan upbringing, and
Holden Caulfield's failure to perform with a whore in Salinger's *The
Catcher in the Rye* taken as evidence of his compassion, but those
explanations are only euphemisms for the conventions of sentimentality. Even when sexual contact does occur (as it increasingly has
in recent literature) it is less a passage to maturity than an acted-
out masturbation fantasy.

Until recently, real initiation in the American novel has been the
result of violence, not of sex. In an almost exclusively masculine
rite of passage, which takes place in the men's club environment of
the wilderness under the tutelage of an old Negro or Indian, the
boy kills "some woodland totem" by which "he enters into a communion of guilt with the natural world in which hitherto he has
led the privileged existence of an outsider." Although this theme
has been most frequently identified with Hemingway and Faulkner
(who, in "The Bear," made his backwoods mentor *both* an Indian
and a Negro), it has also become a stock theme in popular outdoor
fiction. "The boy with 'buck fever,' the kid trembling over the
broken body of his first rabbit or the first bird brought down with
a sling, is the equivalent in the world of violence to the queasy
stripling over the whore's bed in the world of passion" (*CE,* 1:501).

Lately, sentimentality has had to make room for (if not entirely
give way to) less genteel forms of romanticism. Thus, more insidious
images of the child have begun to challenge the maudlin stereotypes
of earlier times. One of the more bizarre examples of this phenomenon is the way in which the sexual innocence of the child has been
championed by Gothic-homosexual novelists of the post-Faulknerian
South. The typical child figure for such a novelist (Fiedler mentions
Carson McCullers and Truman Capote by name) is "ambiguous,
epicene, caught at the indeterminate point where the charm of the
boy and girl are scarcely distinguishable." The most familiar of these

figures is the protagonist of Carson McCullers's *The Member of the Wedding:* "the Good Bad Boy as Teen-age Tomboy, Huck Finn as F. Jasmine Adams." (But then, Fiedler reminds us, Huck had once played the girl.) What has not changed from Twain's earlier fable is the presence of "the Negro, . . . still providing comfort for these transvestite Hucks in their moments of misery; though Jim, too, has been transformed from male to female" (*CE*, 1:504).

In the work of some modern writers, however, the myth of childhood innocence has been abandoned altogether. The two principal characters of Henry James's *The Turn of the Screw* are children "through whom the satanic attempts to enter the adult world" (*CE*, 1:506). (This same notion would later be vulgarized in William Peter Blatty's *The Exorcist.*) In Vladimir Nabokov's *Lolita* we have not a redemptive Good Good Girl, but a twelve-year-old nymphet who seduces a middle-aged man (this motif has long been vulgarized in the underground cult of child pornography). Finally, in William Golding's *The Lord of the Flies,* the parable of man's fall from Eden is reenacted by an all-child society stranded on a desert island.

If the child represents the instinctive self, the id, then it must possess diabolic as well as angelic possibilities. The writers who have realized this "have come to believe that the self can be betrayed to impulse as well as to rigor; that an Age of Innocence can be a tyranny no less terrible than an Age of Reason; and that the Gods of such an age if not yet dead must be killed, however snub-nosed, freckled-faced, or golden-haired they may be" (*CE*, 1:511). Can infant damnation be far behind? Saint Augustine, call your office.

## Chapter Four

# In Place and Time

By far the most enduring literary typologies are those of place and time. Despite the efforts of formalist critics to evaluate and classify texts in strictly aesthetic terms, our college catalogs and standard anthologies still tend to honor the categories of national (or even regional) provenance and historical period (usually defined by the dates of a war). Because of his antiformalist bias, Fiedler is not about to repudiate literary history and geography; however, his approach to these subjects is predictably more speculative than that of the conventional scholar-squirrel.

## Montana on My Mind

In *The Return of the Vanishing American,* Fiedler asserts that "geography in the United States is mythological." Hence, much of our literature has "tended to define itself—topologically, as it were, in terms of the four cardinal directions: a mythicized North, South, East, and West" (*R,* 16). This tendency toward literary regionalism was no doubt a function of the geographical immensity of the American continent. Unlike Europe, America was a big land with a short history. Consequently, it is possible to think of our novels (and to a lesser extent our other genres) as being Northerns, Southerns, Easterns, and Westerns.

The Northern is best exemplified by the novels of William Dean Howells (particularly *The Landlord at Lion's Head*) as well as a little of Henry James—for example, *The Bostonians*—and, "supereminently, Edith Wharton's *Ethan Frome*" (*R,* 17). This type of story "tends to be tight, gray, low-keyed, underplayed, avoiding melodrama where possible—sometimes, it would seem, at all costs. Typically, its scene is domestic, an isolated household set in a hostile environment. The landscape is mythicized New England, 'stern and rock-bound,' the weather deep winter: a milieu appropriate to the austerities and deprivations of Puritanism" (*R,* 16). Such a world seems to come off less well in prose fiction than in the narrative poetry of Robert Frost, Edwin Arlington Robinson, and (more recently) Robert Lowell. Perhaps its supreme embodiment, however, was in Henry David Thoreau's extended prose poem *Walden*.

In contrast to the icy reserve of the Northern, the Southern is a blood-hot genre which actively seeks melodrama. To Fiedler's mind, the Southern is an indigenously American form of Gothic. The ruined mansions of Europe have simply been replaced by the decaying plantation house (because he was an antebellum Southerner, Poe had to set his horrors in "a mythicized Europe"). Moreover, "what the Church and feudal aristocracy were for European Gothic, the Negro became for the American variety" (*R,* 18).[1]

What makes the Southern perhaps the most successful of our topological fictions is its ability to function equally well as highbrow literature ("Edgar Allan Poe through William Faulkner to Truman Capote or Flannery O'Connor") and as mass entertainment (beginning again with Poe and running through to those narratives that Fiedler would later dub specimens of "the inadvertent epic": Thomas Dixon, Jr.'s *The Clansman,* re-created as D. W. Griffith's *The Birth of a Nation,* and Margaret Mitchell's *Gone With the Wind,* as both novel and movie). "The Southern has always challenged the distinction between High and Pop Art, since not merely Poe, its founder, but such latter-day successors of his as Faulkner and Capote [and, one might add, Tennessee Williams] have thrived in the two presumably sundered worlds of critical esteem and mass approval" (*R,* 18).

Far from trying to bridge the gap between canonical and popular literature, the typical Eastern tends to be self-consciously elitist. "Basic to that worship of High Art," Fiedler writes, "was the dogma that there are some books, in fiction chiefly those of James . . . , an appreciation of which distinguishes the elect from the vulgar, the sensitive from the gross, and that those books can be known immediately because a) they are set in Europe, b) they mention other works of art, often so casually that only the cognoscenti know them without the aid of footnotes, and c) they are written by expatriates" (*R,* 20–21).[2] What is at work here is a reversal of the American Adam's movement west. By returning to the sophisticated, decadent, Old World environment of Europe the American is able to appear more "innocent" than in his native habitat. It is thus as a tourist that the American is most identifiably American (in these days of cut-rate air fares, Daisy Miller has been replaced by the gawking suburbanite, with loud shirt, louder children, and ubiquitous camera).

The regional subgenre that has held the greatest fascination for Fiedler (and probably for Americans in general) is the Western. It embodies what is at once the most familiar and most elusive of the topological myths. To Europeans, the West was originally coextensive with the entire New World. (Indeed, by discovering America Columbus gave to the European imagination the concept of the West with which to replace the nightmare image of dragons and sea monsters lurking at the boundaries of a flat earth.) With the settling of the American continent, however, each region that had once been considered west in turn became east. Thus the West that Columbus discovered finally became a mirage, one that ultimately leads us back east to Asia. It is, in the words of Walt Whitman, a "passage to India." Both the oldest and the newest of our mythic regions, the West is simultaneously everywhere and nowhere.

When Fiedler speaks of the West, however, he is not thinking of California (which Theodore Roosevelt aptly characterized as "west of the West"), but of the region between the Mississippi River and the Rocky Mountains. "The heart of the Western is not the confrontation with the alien landscape (by itself this produces only the Northern), but the encounter with the Indian, that utter stranger for whom our New World is an Old Home" (R, 21). Because of the radically strange and alien nature of the Indian, he is the one element of the American experience that white Europeans have never been able to assimilate. Whether he is a survivor of the Lost Continent of Atlantis, a remnant of the wandering tribes of Israel, or some extraterrestrial being, he is the ultimate other. He may have a soul, but—as D. H. Lawrence concluded—"*not* one precisely like our own, except as our own have the potentiality of becoming like his" (R, 22).

According to Fiedler's definition, "the Western" refers neither to a region nor to a direction, but to our encounter with the savage other. "So long as a single untamed Indian inhabits it, any piece of American space can become to the poet's imagination an authentic West" (R, 26). Of course, the corollary of this notion is that once the Indian has disappeared as a mythic presence in the American imagination, the Western will become a defunct genre (a fate which already seems to have befallen the Northern and the Eastern).[3] And yet, the Western is so deeply embedded in our national subconscious that it refuses to go gentle into that good night. It is constantly being redeemed from two directions: from the past in the form of historical fiction (even of the debunking variety such as Thomas Berger's *Little Big Man*); and from the future in the form of science fiction tales, which are really crypto-westerns, "space operas" instead of "horse operas."[4]

During the two decades that he lived in Montana, nothing that Fiedler wrote stirred more local controversy than his essay "Montana; or the End of Jean-Jacques Rousseau." Although few of Fiedler's neighbors read the *Partisan Review*, where it appeared, those who did quickly spread the word that this Eastern ingrate (in the South he would have been called a carpetbagger) was biting "the fine, generous Western hand that was feeding" him (*CE*, 2:331). A university freshman who had been forced by one of Fiedler's colleagues to read the essay told his teacher "that he knew all about the author of this lying 'story,' an Easterner who considered himself too good to talk to anyone and who made his children call him 'sir'!" (*CE*, 2:332).

What was even more disconcerting to Fiedler than the pique of Montana chauvinists was the smugness of disaffected Westerners who considered him a fellow debunker (they would "pluck me by the sleeve to tell me in whispers how many men Calamity Jane slept with and what she charged") and the condescension of "self-satisfied Easterners, who are shocked to discover that I still live in Montana, and look at me with pity and admiration for daring to live among the surly natives I have offended" (*CE*, 2:332).

Fiedler's own feeling was that he was simply engaged in a family quarrel with his adopted home. For this reason he advises civic boosters "to pray nightly that Montana *never* produce a first-rate writer." He remembers Faulkner's being asked by a young lady from Missoula if "So-and-So might someday write the Great Montana Novel, since 'he loved the state so much!' " To this the Nobel laureate replied: " 'To write about a place well, you must *hate* it!' And after a pause, he added, 'The way a man hates his wife' " (*CE*, 2:333).

Fiedler begins his notorious essay by identifying three stages in the development of the frontier. In the first stage the struggle for survival is so intense that the settlers have neither sufficient time nor energy to contemplate the hideous contradiction between their romantic dream of utopia and the barrenness of their present surroundings. However, when the schoolmarm moves out from the

East, displaces the whore, and marries the rancher; "the Dream and the fact confront each other openly." This confrontation results in the perceived need "for some kind of art to nurture the myth, to turn a way of life into a culture" (CE, 1:133). Consequently, the West is reinvented in terms of a sentimentalized image of the frontier purveyed in pulp novels, Western movies, and fake cowboy songs. At the time that Fiedler was writing, Montana was coming to the end of this second phase of frontier development and moving into a third.

This most recent transformation exploits the images of pop art for purely commercial purposes. It brings us the West of the dude ranch and the Chamber of Commerce rodeo. In effect, popular mythology has become so powerful and so pervasive that life not only begins to imitate art, but also to forget that any discrepancy exists between the two: "Certainly for the bystander watching the cowboy, a comic book under his arm, lounging beneath the bright poster of the latest Roy Rogers film, there is the sense of a joke on someone—and no one to laugh. It is nothing less than the total myth of the goodness of man in a state of nature that is at stake every Saturday after the show at the Rialto; and, though there is scarcely anyone who sees the issue clearly or as a whole, most Montanans are driven instinctively to try to close the gap" (CE, 1:136).

The degeneration of the frontier dream was probably inevitable. In the past, men would simply discard a failed utopia by pushing west in search of a new frontier. But since Montana is on the last frontier, geographical eschatology has given way to fantasy. The real cowboy imaginatively re-creates himself as Roy Rogers, while the upper-class Montanan identifies with an even older prototype of frontier nobility—the pioneer and mountain man (e.g., Jim Bridger or John Colter). Some who are of a liberal or romantic sensibility even try to redeem the image of the Indian as Noble Savage without really coming to terms with the presence of today's Indian "despised and outcast in his open-air ghettos" (CE, 1:141).

Fiedler concludes by urging his fellow Montanans to make the painful but necessary adjustment from myth to reality: "When he admits that the Noble Savage is a lie; when he has learned that his state is where the myth comes to die (it is here, one is reminded, that the original of Huck Finn ended his days, a respected citizen), the Montanan may find the possibilities of tragedy and poetry for which so far he has searched his life in vain" (CE, 1:141).

## The Way We Were

If the American West is the place that has most deeply engaged Fiedler's imagination, the period with which he most closely identifies is the 1930s. This was, of course, the time of his own adolescence, when his literary sensibility was being shaped. In writing about the thirties from the perspective of the late sixties, he not only stresses the affinities between these two eras, but also points out the discrepancies between the official history of an age and those things which seem most essential to the actual survivors of that age. Appropriately, he calls his essay "The Two Memories: Reflections on Writers and Writing in the Thirties."

At one level, the notion of literary periods is as arbitrary as that of literary regions; however, it is possible to speak of the dominant myths of particular times even if those myths do not change like clockwork with the passing of each decade. "The Radicalism of the sixties, like that of the thirties," Fiedler writes, "is influenced by the Bohemia which preceded it, and with which it remains uncomfortably entangled; and it differs from its earlier counterpart precisely as the one Bohemia differs from the other" (*CE*, 2:238–39). What makes the situation even more complex and paradoxical is that one of the principal legacies that the Bohemia of the fifties bequeathed to the radicals of the sixties was the "memory" of an underground thirties fundamentally different from the overtly political era represented by the likes of Dos Passos and Steinbeck (both of whom had turned to the right by the sixties).

When Jerry Rubin suggested that the Yippies had more in common with Groucho Marx than with Karl, he was making the salient distinction between a programmatic revolution and an anarchic one. It does not take an excessive flight of fancy to make the connection between S. J. Perelman (scenarist of several Marx Brothers films) and Perelman's brother-in-law Nathanael West. Although nominally a leftist, West was actually an absurdist and con man whose bleak existentialist vision was at odds with the political millenialism of his time. During his life, he was a virtually unknown novelist who supported himself by cranking out B movie scripts. It was not until the late fifties that his novels were brought back into print, perhaps because it took the era of the bomb to make West's cynical foretaste of apocalypse seem credible. His reputation was revived by the Beats of the fifties and enhanced by literate radicals of the sixties.

The one figure who dominates the official history of the thirties but who is strangely absent from the literature of that period is Franklin D. Roosevelt. Despite the New Deal affiliations of middlebrow writers such as Archibald McLeish and Robert E. Sherwood, Roosevelt was considered largely irrelevant by nihilists such as West and positively dangerous by more revolutionary leftists (although he has always been the bête noire of the right, it is at least arguable that Roosevelt saved capitalism from its own excesses). According to Whittaker Chambers, Alger Hiss took pleasure "in the most simple and brutal references to the President's physical condition as a symbol of the middle class breakdown." To Fiedler, "the implicit metaphor is clear enough: F.D.R. as Lady Chatterley's impotent husband, the C.P. as her prepotent lover, and the American working class as Constance herself " (*CE*, 2:242).

In a much different context, Garry Wills has written: "Winners erect their own monuments, while losers ache with music."[5] Such is the case with the thirties that Fiedler remembers. If Roosevelt and the New Deal were official monuments of the period, its music (i.e., song and story) commemorates a series of lost causes: Sacco and Vanzetti, the Scottsboro Boys, and—most of all—the Spanish Civil War. While Roosevelt embargoed arms to the Loyalists (as a means of securing the Catholic vote), thousands of Americans volunteered for the losing battle against fascism. As Fiedler reminds us, "it was especially a war which captured the imagination of writers everywhere" (*CE*, 2:247). For Jewish and left-wing intellectuals of the thirties, the war in Spain was what the American Civil War had been to the South—a glorious defeat against which the spoils of any possible victory pale in comparison.

Also at work in the thirties was an older generation of writers, consisting largely of former expatriates who had now returned to their homeland (a phenomenon chronicled in Malcolm Cowley's *Exile's Return*). The experience of these writers suggests that expatriation reveals the sham of the Eastern myth. For them the journey west was also the journey home. One American expatriate who was just starting to come into his own during the sixties was Henry Miller. Like West, Miller was a writer out of place during the thirties who was fortunate enough to be discovered by a later generation of readers. With the lifting of the ban on his controversial masterpiece *The Tropic of Cancer,* Miller made "the difficult transition from a cult favorite, smuggled past customs into the land of his birth, to a popular author, displayed on newsstands in airports and supermarkets" (*WE*, 40). In *Waiting for the End,* Fiedler casts a critical eye at this late canonization of Henry Miller.

Essentially, Fiedler accuses Miller of having raised immaturity to the level of a metaphysical principle. Lacking a tragic sense, he uses his gift for comedy to spread gossip and to betray his friends: "In the very moment that Miller tells us how he rewarded by sleeping with their wives those who sponsored, clothed, fed, and subsidized him, he is further rewarding them by making a comic tale of that betrayal or by drawing comic portraits of the sex organs of those wives, thus compounding the initial treachery" (*WE*, 43). What makes the Miller persona even more intolerable is its smug celebration of adolescent self-indulgence. Although this personality trait is characteristically American, Miller is not "an American in the line of Hawthorne, Melville, and Faulkner . . . , but rather a late link in the chain that begins with Benjamin Franklin and passes through Emerson to Mary Baker Eddy: the line of self-congratulatory post-Christians who manufactured homegrown religions (often with hints of the mysterious East) to express their assurance that tragedy was an illusion and death was not real" (*WE*, 44).

Although the radical and avant-garde literature of the thirties constitutes the tradition with which Fiedler is most familiar, he recognizes (as many commentators do not) that there was a very different but equally powerful literary movement under way at approximately the same time in the American South. If contemporary Jewish novelists such as Saul Bellow were influenced by the literature of the radical thirties, other contemporary writers (Fiedler mentions Truman Capote and the expatriated Canadian Marshal McLuhan) were nurtured by the contemporaneous Agrarian tradition.

In addition to the most obvious regional and ethnic differences, the radical and Agrarian thirties were separated by fundamentally opposite myths. The radical vision existed in the tension between "the terrible fact of the present and the dream of a barely possible pure future" (*CE*, 2:258). In contrast, the Agrarians were caught between "an equally dismal actuality and the dream of a manifestly unreal pure past." "Nonetheless," Fiedler argues, "the manifestos of the Agrarians tell the kind of lie which illuminates the truth of the fiction of Faulkner and Warren and Bishop, even as the Marxist manifestos tell the kind of lie which illuminates the truth of the novels of Nathanael West and Henry Roth" (*CE*, 2:258–59).

The primary statement of Agrarian philosophy—a symposium belligerently entitled *I'll Take My Stand*—was a consciously reactionary response to the cultural assimilation of the South into the mainstream of American society. Oftentimes, a settled way of life becomes accessible to the literary imagination only when it is in the process of dying. The dramatic conflict inherent in a transformation of cultures can produce a tragic and elegiac literature. *I'll Take My Stand* was itself too dogmatic and too polemical to generate a truly introspective literature; however, the forces that made Agrarianism inevitable also gave rise to the Southern modernism of Faulkner and company. One of the most underrated members of that company, according to Fiedler, was West Virginia native John Peale Bishop.

In making the claim that Bishop was "perhaps the most important Southern novelist of the thirties," Fiedler acknowledges that most readers who are familiar with Bishop "associate him with a different genre, a different decade, even a different region" (*CE*, 2:259). A Princeton classmate of Edmund Wilson and Scott Fitzgerald (he was the model for Tom d'Invilliers in *This Side of Paradise*), Bishop is known primarily as a cosmopolitan poet of the twenties. He was also one of the first writers of the Southern Renaissance to remove himself from the South (living as a permanent expatriate in Paris). However, he kept in touch with his native region by maintaining a lifelong correspondence with Allen Tate; and in his single completed novel, *Act of Darkness* (1935), Bishop returned to the setting and mythic preoccupations of the American South.

*Act of Darkness* concerns the trial of a West Virginia gentleman who has raped a middle-aged Southern lady. Because the crime is not an interracial assault, it would seem to be an anomaly in Southern fiction. Indeed, "such a gentleman farmer as the Agrarians were then making the focus of their hopes for social reform is responsible, at least passively, for the act of darkness which the color of his skin seems to belie" (*CE*, 2:267). The rapist's nephew, who had idolized his uncle and is shattered by the recent turn of events, experiences a rather surprising epiphany when reading Shakespeare's *Othello*. Subscribing to the theory that Othello was not black but a Venetian nobleman named Il Moro (who "had, in the repetition of the story of the murder of his wife, been mistaken for a Moor" [see *CE*, 2:269]), the nephew realizes that the nightmare image of the Negro rapist is no more than a projection of what lies within each of us.

This knowledge enables the boy to leave the South, after a visit to the local whorehouse where he accomplishes the consummation that he had previously fumbled. There he is oddly enough sustained by his uncle's contention that it was his victim who actually raped *him*. This means, according to Fiedler, "that the true Othello is Desdemona: the pale virgin dreaming her own dark violation, and projecting that dream outward upon the white male who resents her" (*CE*, 2:269). In his verse Bishop had already conceived of the poetic act as the joining of elegance and force (*pudeur* and *chutzpah*?) symbolized by the marriage of Desdemona and Othello. By virtue of dramatizing this image of the poet cum black man cum everyman, *Act of Darkness* may well be the ultimate meta-Southern novel.

## Chapter Five
# Eros and Thanatos

In a 1984 interview Leslie Fiedler observed: "The typical pattern with one of my books . . . is that when it comes out everybody abuses it. Ten years later they're still abusing it but they've begun to steal ideas from it. Twenty years go by and they decide it is a classic, although nobody's ever said anything good about it."[1] Whether or not this is the typical pattern for one of Fiedler's books, it has certainly been the fate of his magnum opus, *Love and Death in the American Novel* (1960; revised edition, 1966). The book scandalized conventional pedants by its absence of footnotes and bibliography, and distressed formalist critics by its unabashed eclecticism (writing in *Partisan Review,* John Raleigh complained that the book "is neither criticism nor history nor sociology nor psychology but is rather a kind of amateur brand of sociology *cum* sex, or, rather, sex *cum* sociology").[2] Yet as the years have passed, *Love and Death* has joined only a handful of other books (in American Studies one thinks of F. O. Matthiessen's *American Renaissance* and R. W. B. Lewis's *The American Adam*) as a permanent fixture on Ph.D. reading lists.

## American Gothic

The concept of the "great American novel" is itself an implicit confession that prose fiction is the literary form best suited to the American experience. In large part this is a function of history. For economic and social reasons well documented by Ian Watt and others, the modern novel came into being with the rise of capitalism and the middle class in eighteenth-century England. Because this was precisely the time when America was developing a national identity, it is not surprising that the new genre was readily adopted by the New World. In the first half of his study Fiedler concentrates on the way in which European prototypes were altered in the evolution of a distinctively American novel.

The three basic paradigms available to eighteenth-century American novelists were the Richardsonian tale of seduction, the pseudo-Shakespearean epic of Fielding, and the Gothic romance of Monk Lewis. The first of these became the province of female sentimentalists whose popular success has always exceeded their critical acclaim. The second "with its broad canvas, its emphasis upon reversals and recognitions, and its robust masculine sentimentality, turned out, oddly enough, to have no relevance to the American scene" (*LD*, 28).[3] What has come to be regarded as "classic" American literature (a concept that Fiedler later repudiated as elitist) can be seen as a variation on the Gothic. "Our fiction," Fiedler writes, "is essentially and at its best nonrealistic, even anti-realistic; long before *symbolisme* had been invented in France and exported to America, there was a full-fledged native tradition of symbolism" (*LD*, 28–29). It is this tradition that is the focus of *Love and Death in the American Novel.*

Before discussing the Gothic canon of American fiction, however, Fiedler traces the history of the novel's emergence in England and its transplantation to America. The point that he stresses throughout is the popular, bourgeois, individualistic nature of the novel. The genre arose as a reaction to the class-conscious literature of court and salon, was dependent upon mass production and a middle-class audience for its very existence, and was not even considered high art until the age of Flaubert and Henry James. Moreover, Fiedler reminds us that "the moment at which the novel took hold coincides with the moment of the sexual division of labor which left business to the male, the arts to the female—thus laying up for the future the perils of Bovaryism, on the one hand, and on the other, the dictatorship of 'what the young girl wants' or, perhaps better, what her father thinks she *should* want" (*LD*, 42).

According to Fiedler, there were three levels of duplicity involved in the rise of the bourgeois novel: it represented the marvelous as ordinary, passion as piety, and entertainment as moral instruction. These evasions can be explained sociologically by the Puritan aversion to art and fancy. While literature was not totally outlawed, it had to be smuggled into the parlor in the guise of a sermon. The faith it served, however, was not that of Milton's stern Puritan despot, but rather "that secret religion of the bourgeoisie in which tears are considered a truer service of God than prayers, the Pure Young Girl replaces Christ as the savior, marriage becomes the equivalent of bliss eternal, and the Seducer is the only Devil" (LD, 45). In Fiedler's opinion, this religion of sentimental love is simply the Protestant manifestation of a process that had been developing in the Western psyche since at least the late Middle Ages.

Like the emergence of courtly love (and the more extreme forms of Mariolatry) in eleventh-century Europe, the evolution of the bourgeois novel represented "the irruption of the female principle into a patriarchal world, a revenge of the (officially rejected) Great Mother" (LD, 47). In the Catholic Mediterranean countries, the orthodox trinity of Father, Son, and Holy Ghost was enshrined in dogma; while the baroque trinity of cuckold, mother, and son was worshipped in art. By the same token, "it was on the religious marches of Europe, where mother-directed Catholicism and father-centered Protestantism met, in France, Germany, and England, that the novel especially flourished. . . . Committed to the Northern rejection of the Virgin, such men [as Richardson and Goethe] sought with special urgency to smuggle the mother principle back into their cultures. They were thus specially qualified to satisfy the secret hunger of the puritanical bourgeoisie, which demanded bootleg madonnas; it was the function of the early novel to supply them" (LD, 56).

Given the proper social conditions and a receptive mind-set, it required only a model narrative for the sentimental love religion to become myth for the Protestant middle class. Samuel Richardson (who is credited by many with having invented the novel) actually provided complementary narratives—one comic and one tragic— in Pamela and Clarissa. Both involve a confrontation between an unprincipled seducer and a virginal young girl. In Pamela the heroine maintains her purity and is rewarded with marriage to the morally chastened aristocrat who had sought her favors illicitly. As Fiedler emphasizes, virginity is not itself a thing of value in the bourgeois worldview, but rather a quality that makes the young woman worthy of the ultimate social good—marriage to someone of a higher station. And if anyone should miss the underlying commercial ethic (which, in Fiedler's apt phrase, makes Pamela a "female Ben Franklin"), Richardson has subtitled his novel "Virtue Rewarded."

Although it is not as widely read as Pamela, Clarissa is perhaps even more potent as a mythic paradigm. Here, the Don Juan figure is not a roguish hero, nor is he finally made to capitulate to the bourgeois respectability of marriage. In the conflict of the chaste

Clarissa and the rapacious Lovelace, we have a meeting of the immovable object with the irresistible force. Refusing willingly to give into Lovelace's overtures, Clarissa is drugged and violated. Nevertheless, she maintains the purity of her soul and dies a long, agonizing death. The blackguard Lovelace subsequently expires in a duel, but not before having a vision of Clarissa in Heaven and himself in Hell. This final vision blatantly exposes the Manichaeanism of the sentimental love religion. Although His name is often invoked, there is no supreme being here: "there are only man and woman in eternal conflict; for the divine principle has been subsumed in the female even as the diabolic has been in the male" (*LD*, 67).

The Richardsonian prototypes survived in American literature and maintained a presence throughout the nineteenth century. The narrative in which they were originally embodied, however, lacked mythic power when it was transferred to an American setting. As Fiedler notes: "It is impossible to contrast domestic virtues with courtly ones in a country where there has never been a court, so that the essential Richardsonian conflict, which is also the dialectic of the form, is inevitably lost" (*LD*, 76). What has not been lost is the notion of female chastity as the apotheosis of virtue and the image of the suffering female herself as vicarious Christ—redeeming the penitent sinner (as in *Pamela*) or damning the impenitent one (as in *Clarissa*) by the purity of her example. These attitudes were consistent with the Puritan repudiation of overt sexual desire; however, they would not have achieved their specific form if the secularized sentimentality that was fast replacing Puritan theology had not also supplanted the patriarchal God of the old religion with a new feminine anima.

Although one can find numerous variations of Clarissa in the high canon of American literature, her most obvious presence is in the popular novel. The sad fate of the wronged maiden was a stock theme in pulp tearjerkers well into our own century (until the sexual revolution made that theme passé). Viewing sexual violation from the other side of the bed were pornographers who pruriently depicted the act of seduction itself (pornography simply being the dark side of sentimentality). Since women in American fiction generally lacked the moral and physical stamina of Clarissa, those who maintained their virtue were either saved melodramatically from the buzzsaw by a dashing young hero or—like the Good Good Girl—dispatched from this vale of tears before the onset of puberty.

As we have previously noted, Fiedler finds the most enduring
and formative influence in American fiction to be not the Richardsonian novel of seduction but the Gothic romance. In moving from
the Richardsonian to the Gothic narrative, we find that terror has
replaced love as the essential theme of fiction: "The titillation of
sex denied, [the Gothic romance] offers its readers a vicarious par-
ticipation in a flirtation with death—approach and retreat, approach
and retreat, the fatal orgasm eternally mounting and eternally
checked" (LD, 134). Moreover, there are crucial formal differences
between the sentimental and the Gothic tale. To begin with, the
setting of Clarissa's flight is society, while that of the Gothic heroine
is "out of the known world into a dark region of make-believe"
(LD, 128). Also, in tone and emphasis, the Gothic mode forswears
the belief in light and redemption found in the sentimental novel,
stressing instead the power of darkness and damnation. Finally, the
smug sense of bourgeois innocence and probity that underlies the
Richardsonian world view is replaced by a brooding sense of guilt
and anxiety.

There were clear problems, however, in transferring the Gothic
romance from Europe to America. Although the image of the maiden
in flight and the figure of the ambiguous hero-villain presented no
difficulties, there were no haunted castles in the New World nor
any established class system to provide the historical and social
background on which European Gothicism thrived. What was needed
was a set of indigenous symbols that would evoke a distinctively
American sense of Gothic terror. The man who would discover (or
invent) this set of symbols was the first important American novelist,
Charles Brockden Brown. Whether or not his own work is finally
judged a success, Brown created the romantic image of the American
writer and, through his influence on Poe and Hawthorne, helped
to shape the course of American fiction.

In his detailed discussion of *Edgar Huntley* and briefer comments
on Brown's other novels, Fiedler shows that the newly created American Gothic replaced the haunted castle and the dungeon with the
haunted forest and the cave or natural abyss. This involved not just
a change of medium but also of message. In the American Gothic,
it was nature itself, not the decaying monuments of a dying civilization, that became the symbol of evil. Fiedler points out that
"similarly not the aristocrat but the Indian, not the dandified cour-
tier but the savage colored man is postulated as the embodiment of

villainy" (*LD,* 160). Whereas the European Gothic was revolutionary in its identification of darkness with the superego, the American
Gothic of Charles Brockden Brown was essentially conservative—
even Calvinist—in its linking of evil with the id. Within his grand
scheme, Fiedler sees this view of nature and the savage as the dialectical opposite of a Rousseauistic tradition in American fiction,
one that was first elevated to the realm of myth in the novels of
James Fenimore Cooper.

Just as Brown adapted the Gothic novel to the American scene,
Cooper remade the historical romance in the image of the New
World. Although it is sometimes regarded as a subgenre of the
Gothic (both are concerned with the past and with making the
marvelous credible), the historical romance represents a crucial difference in outlook. For those writing in the tradition of Cooper and
Sir Walter Scott, the savage and primitive are purged of their demonic associations and sometimes even established as moral norms.
Like the Gothicist, the "white romantic" is fascinated by the quaint
and picturesque, but his attitude is more likely to be one of nostalgia
than of horror. In the historical novel, "hero and heroine flee not
projections of their feared inner selves but real enemies, genuine
conspiracies, external dangers. . . . The historical Romance (and
its companion form, the Romantic narrative poem as practiced by
Byron) represents the sight-seeing of the middle classes before cheap
and speedy transportation had made it possible for them to do it
in the flesh" (*LD,* 163).

By appropriating the landscape of the Gothic novel, the plot and
theme of the historical romance, and some of the character types of
the Richardsonian tale of seduction, Cooper was a great synthesizer
of adult literary traditions. As Fiedler notes, however, those works
of his that continue to live tend to be regarded as children's (or
more specifically boy's) books. This is a fate that Cooper's Leatherstocking Tales shares with the first two parts of *Gulliver's Travels,*
*Robinson Crusoe,* some of Scott (e.g., *Ivanhoe*), and Dickens (e.g.,
*Oliver Twist*), and much of Robert Louis Stevenson (e.g., *Treasure
Island* and *David Balfour*). These books have certain characteristics
in common: "all of them have male protagonists, adult or juvenile;
all involve adventure and isolation plus an escape at one point or
another, or a flight from society to an island, a woods, the under-
world, a mountain fastness—some place at least where mothers do
not come; most all of them involve, too, a male companion, who

is the spirit of the alien place, and who is presented with varying degrees of ambiguity as helpmate and threat" *(LD,* 181). That such a pattern would be repeated again and again in classic American novels is a point that Fiedler has been making ever since he published "Come Back to the Raft Ag'in, Huck Honey!" in the June 1948 issue of *Partisan Review.*

In this, his best-known and most controversial essay, Fiedler observes that at the center of our classic novel, we do not find the European preoccupation with adult heterosexual passion, but rather a flight from petticoat government. Our great novels are boy's books because American men are to a large extent boys at heart. An essential aspect of our sentimental life is "the camaraderie of the locker room and ball park, the good fellowship of the poker game and fishing trip, a kind of passionless passion, at once gross and delicate, homoerotic in the boy's sense, possessing an innocence above suspicion" *(CE,* 1:143). (Underlying this macho utopia is the fear of overt homosexuality as a threat to the mythic chastity of male companionship.)

Although the refugee from matriarchal civilization is occasionally isolated (as was Thoreau at Walden), more often there is a wilderness bonding between males. The central enduring relationship in our literature, this bonding is a pure antimarriage, because it is freed of the complications of sexual passion and of the responsibilities of domestic life. In a world without women, it is possible to enjoy both freedom and community—even if it is only the community of a boy and a runaway slave floating downriver on a raft.

What makes this theme of male bonding more complex (and seemingly at odds with the official mores of American society) is that it frequently joins a white and a colored man. The most famous (though hardly exclusive) examples are to be found in the Leatherstocking Tales (Natty Bumppo and Chingachgook), *Moby-Dick* (Ishmael and Queequeg), and *Adventures of Huckleberry Finn* (Huck and Jim). When the white man (or boy) dreams himself a renegade from society, he is symbolically joined to that alien other who has always (as if by definition) been a renegade. It should not be surprising, then, that the dream finds its embodiment in our most mythically resonant literature. Nevertheless, our social taboos are such that it has usually been foreigners (e.g., Lawrence and Lorca) who have guessed the truth. At the very least, it was a breach of etiquette for an insider such as Fiedler to expose this archetype at the heart of the American experience.

Because the more widely accepted myth of race relations in America is one of heterosexual rape (most often the simian darky violating the pure Southern belle, as in Dixon's *The Clansman* and Griffith's *The Birth of a Nation,* but sometimes the diabolic slave owner mounting his helpless black wench, as in Stowe's *Uncle Tom's Cabin* and Haley's *Roots*), the innocent vision of interracial male love is deeply subversive. Unfortunately, the tactlessness of Fiedler's vocabulary caused many early readers to miss the point that he was making. Philip Rahv, who published "Come Back to the Raft" in the *Partisan Review,* later insisted that he had done so only because he thought it a clever put-on.[4] Others simply concluded that Fiedler believed Huck and Jim quite literally to be "queer as three-dollar bills" (*WWL,* 15). What the essay actually said was more complicated and profound. In essence, it is this: "Behind the white American's nightmare that someday, no longer tourist, inheritor, or liberator, he will be rejected, refused, he dreams of his acceptance at the breast he has most utterly offended. It is a dream so sentimental, so outrageous, so desperate that it redeems our concept of boyhood from nostalgia to tragedy" (*CE,* 1:151).

The archetype of interethnic male bonding first makes its appearance in American literature in the figures of Natty and Chingachgook. From the time of Cooper on, the prototypical American hero (particularly in the pulp Western) has shunned both women *and* civilization as a single threat to his freedom. In *The Last of the Mohicans,* Natty (who is here known as Hawkeye) suggests rather unconvincingly that his lack of desire for the opposite sex is due to his unfamiliarity with society and its conventions of courtship. Later on, he asserts that the bond that joins him to Uncas is stronger than that which unites man and wife. Then, after the death of Uncas, he renews his vow of fealty to Chingachgook. As Fiedler notes, the culturally plausible expedient of mating Natty with an Indian squaw is prevented by Cooper's implacable fear of miscegenation (an obsession he shared with the creators of the "inadvertent epic").

If Cooper represents the chaste male couple of the wilderness novel in the characters of Natty and Chingachgook, he uses the main action of *The Last of the Mohicans* to depict the darker and more pervasive fear of interethnic rape. Although Cooper skirts the issue, it is clear that Magua—the bad Indian—is intent on violating Colonel Munro's daughter Cora. It is just as clear that Cora and the good Indian Uncas are attracted to each other. Rather than transgress the sacred color line, Cooper has both Indians die without possessing their beloved. (Hawkeye will not even allow the Indian mourners the consolation of imagining Cora and Uncas joined in the hereafter.) The crowning irony is that Cora must also be killed off to prevent her from ever mating with a white man (which is no immediate threat, since the matinee idol Duncan Heyward prefers her blonde sister Alice). This is not because Cora is a Good Good Girl whose maidenhead must be preserved at all costs, but because she is the product of her father's liaison with a light-skinned Negress. Insofar as she is white, she cannot have an Indian lover; insofar as she is black, she cannot have a white husband. Thus, in what is ostensibly a historical romance, or only a boy's adventure book, Cooper gave narrative embodiment to what would become our culture's subconscious preoccupation with race and sex.

## Tragic Ambivalence

As one can infer from Fiedler's discussion of Brown and Cooper, the development of the American novel can be seen largely in terms of the adaptation of European models to the circumstances of a radically new environment. The second half of his study is devoted to the later adaptations that have given our classic literature a tradition of its own, different from but continuous with that of our mother country. One such adaptation was Nathaniel Hawthorne's transformation of the Richardsonian tale of seduction into a series of Gothic romances that deal more forthrightly with adult heterosexual passion than any other American fictions prior to James.

In Richardson's fable chastity and suffering were united in the single figure of Clarissa (indeed, it was the preservation of her chastity that caused Clarissa's righteous suffering). In Hawthorne's *The Blithedale Romance* and *The Marble Faun* (and numerous other American narratives), the Clarissa prototype has been divided. The virgin is represented as an ethereal blonde-haired snow maiden (e.g., Priscilla in *The Blithedale Romance* and Hilda in *The Marble Faun*), while the suffering female (e.g., Zenobia in *The Blithedale Romance* and Miriam in *The Marble Faun*) is a dark-haired lady of passion and sensuality. (Hardly original with Hawthorne, this polarity appears in Cooper's *The Last of the Mohicans* in the characters of Alice and Cora Munro.)[5] Although he is too much a child of the Puritans ever to show the dark lady triumphant, Hawthorne generally made her a more interesting figure than her pale opposite (like Milton, he was secretly of the Devil's party).

The one Hawthorne novel from which the snow maiden is completely absent is *The Scarlet Letter*. Here, the sensuous and suffering dark lady exists without a virgin foil. However, Hawthorne stops short of suggesting that feeling is itself redemptive. (Dimmesdale is saved by the confession that brings on his death, and Hester is consigned to the role of Protestant nun.) Moreover, Hawthorne seems to be less interested in passion as such than in its moral consequences and ramifications. The fall of his characters is postulated rather than enacted. Fiedler notes that "Hawthorne is the only American novelist of classic stature who deals centrally in his most important works with the seduction theme; yet there is no seduction scene . . . in any of his works!" (*LD*, 224–25).

After Hawthorne the seduction tale was relegated to popular literature for several decades, only to be revived for "serious" fiction by Stephen Crane and Theodore Dreiser in the guise of naturalism. In his discussion of *Sister Carrie*, Fiedler demonstrates that Dreiser was more a sentimentalist than the libertine he was accused of being. Although he does not kill Carrie off (as Crane had done with Maggie), he shows her come to an ambiguous end and Hurstwood fatally punished for his transgressions. Dreiser shared the bourgeois notion that the loss of virginity was the worst fate that could befall a girl; however, the censors were more concerned with the fact that Dreiser dealt with illicit sex than with the attitude he took toward it. In reality, Dreiser's gingerly treatment of passion is considerably less subversive than his indictment of American society: "What makes *An American Tragedy* particularly American is the fact that Clarissa falls prey not to Lovelace but to Horatio Alger!" (*LD*, 254).

After a discussion of the Good Good Girl and the Good Bad Boy (which is largely, though not exclusively, a recycling of his earlier "Eye of Innocence" essay), Fiedler devotes a chapter to the treatment of women in American fiction. Because the books that he considers were all written by men, this chapter is entitled "The Revenge on Women: From Lucy to Lolita." The point that he makes here is that one of the corollaries of the innocent homoeroticism of the American novel is an inability to deal with women as fully developed, three-dimensional characters (the polarization of women into snow maidens and dark ladies is one symptom of this problem). Although Henry James is frequently cited as a notable exception to this misogynist tradition, his novels are also filled with sexual stereotypes.

Fiedler argues that the conventional dichotomy between virginal and worldly women (complete with appropriate color scheme) is a staple of James's best novels. What James adds is the international slant that identifies the snow maiden as an innocent American and the dark lady as a worldly European (of course, Hawthorne had originated this distinction in *The Marble Faun*), "or more precisely, the American girl who has remained true to her essential Niceness and the American lady who has fallen to the level of European cynicism and moral improvisation" (*LD,* 305). The Jamesian Nice Girl seeks a European husband, not because she wants to escape the moral constraints of her homeland, but because she is eager to share them: "to naturalize her bridegroom to the American ethos, as Clarissa or Pamela had sought once to naturalize their lovers to the world of bourgeois values." Conversely, "the not-quite-nice American girl . . . seeks to yield herself up to Europe and its ways, as do Kate Croy or Charlotte [Temple] or Madame Merle. To Henry James the Fair Maiden, the Good Good Girl is quite simply America itself—her whiteness the outward manifestation of our mysterious national immunity to guilt, which he feels as at once lovely, comic, and quite terrible" (*LD,* 305–6).

In the high literature of our own age the pale virgin has all but disappeared, only to be replaced by her opposite—not the dark lady, but the coquette. The bitch goddess of the twentieth century masquerades as an innocent fair-haired child, but she is not above using her teasing sensuality for personal gain. Unlike the dark lady, she is motivated not by passion but by cold calculation. If James's Fair Maiden represented one image of America, the bitch goddess of F. Scott Fitzgerald symbolized a quite different one. Sharing the first name of James's Daisy Miller, Fitzgerald's Daisy Buchanan is actually "an odd inversion of Clarissa-Charlotte Temple-Maggie Verver; no longer the abused woman, who only by her suffering and death castrates her betrayer, but the abusing woman, symbol of an imperialist rather than a colonial America" (*LD,* 312–13).

Because the bitch is so often dominant in Fitzgerald's fiction, there is a reversal of traditional sex roles. The ingenuous male becomes passive victim of a force he can neither understand nor control. To Fiedler's mind, it is he who is the true descendant of Daisy Miller. Like James's heroine, Jay Gatsby (née Gatz) is "the naïf out of the West destined to shock the upholders of decorum and to die of a love for which there is no worthy object." By making characters such as Gatsby and Dick Diver into embodiments of American innocence, Fitzgerald stands the Richardsonian prototype on its head, "remaking Clarissa in Lovelace's image, Lovelace in Clarissa's" (*LD,* 313).

In Fitzgerald's fictional world we have a mythically realized image of the female, but "little consummated genital love." ("In his insufferable early books," Fiedler writes, "the American institution of *coitus interruptus,* from bundling to necking a favorite national pastime, finds at last a laureate; and even in his more mature works, his women move from the kiss to the kill with only the barest suggestion of copulation between" [*LD,* 316].) With Hemingway, however, we have the opposite situation: he is very fond of depicting the sex act, but has a difficult time conjuring up believable women as partners. Consequently, his sex scenes range from the brutal to the ludicrous. Although he is most at home in the wilderness men's club, Hemingway's particular version of machismo involves frequent sexual conquests. He simply cannot think of anything to do with the woman once the male libido is satisfied.

Like so many of his American predecessors, Hemingway employs the cliché of the dark lady and the fair; however, in his mythology neither is a virgin. The dark lady, who is usually Indian or Latin, is a kind of mindless, subservient geisha girl descended from Melville's Fayaway (the exotic Polynesian consort of Tommo, protagonist of *Typee*). These women are essentially "painless devices for extracting seed without human engagement." Conversely, the Anglo-Saxon woman (whether she is literally blonde or not) is invariably the bitch goddess who uses her allure to assert power over, and thus symbolically castrate, the men in her life. Neither female prototype is much more than a projection of the masculine subconscious. The Anglo-Saxon coquette represents the fear of (or masculine desire for) emasculation; while "through the Dark anti-virgin . . . a new lover enters into a blameless communion with the other uncommitted males who have possessed her and departed, as well as with those yet to come. It is a kind of homosexuality once removed, the appeal of the whorehouse (Eden of the world of men without women) embodied in a single figure" (*LD*, 318).

We find a somewhat different variation of American misogyny in the writings of William Faulkner. With seemingly nothing good to say about white women of childbearing age, Faulkner mythologizes (and some would say sentimentalizes) maternal black women such as Dilsey in *The Sound and the Fury* and Mollie Beauchamp in *Go Down, Moses*—a book dedicated to his own family servant Mammy Caroline Barr. (For Faulkner the dark lady is not an exotic seed extractor, but a surrogate mother.) And yet, in a literary tradition in which the Good Good Girl can grow up to become a bitch goddess, not even motherhood itself is inviolate. From Mary Glendinning in Melville's *Pierre* to Mrs. Ellis Burden in Warren's *All the King's Men* (and one might as well add Sophie Portnoy in Roth's *Portnoy's Complaint*), certain mothers have, through their excessive solicitude, assumed the role of castrating bitch. Literary matricide makes the revenge on women complete.

With women (or more specifically matriarchy) identified as the enemy, the only satisfactory human relationship that is left is between males. This point, which Fiedler has made elsewhere in his writing, is greatly elaborated in *Love and Death,* beginning with a discussion of Rip Van Winkle's flight from petticoat government and moving through a consideration of such disparate latter-day Rips as Hemingway, Faulkner, Dagwood, and Jiggs. It is within this context that Fiedler expands on the more limited theme of interracial homoeroticism. Although *Huckleberry Finn* had supplied the title of his earlier essay, Fiedler finds the Huck-honey motif to be a much more explicit concern of *Moby-Dick.* According to this reading, the love story of Ishmael and Queequeg serves as a foil to the Faustian tragedy of Captain Ahab. Only Melville's great mythopoeic powers redeem the former story from sentimentality and the latter one from melodrama.

Having expatiated at considerable length on eros, Fiedler returns his attention to thanatos in a chapter devoted largely to Poe's contributions to American Gothicism (actually, as the poet laureate of necrophilia, Poe manages to unite eros and thanatos into a single myth). Fiedler's conclusion is that Poe's Gothicism is limited by his failure to deal with the ultimate source of blackness in American literature—the Negro. As more successful counterexamples, he cites the Melville of *Benito Cereno* and the Twain of *Pudd'nhead Wilson*

(*Huck Finn* is interracial, but Nigger Jim is closer to being an Indian in blackface than a Southern Negro; thus making Twain's greatest novel more a Western than a Southern). To Fiedler's mind, Poe's greatest accomplishment in the realm of myth was to create the image of the *poéte maudit* in his own likeness.

One of the more fascinating and controversial arguments that Fiedler makes in *Love and Death* is that the Faust figure has maintained a continuing presence in the American novel. Certainly, Melville's Captain Ahab and Faulkner's Thomas Sutpen (with Flem Snopes as his farcical counterpart) would seem to fit this prototype; however, others whom Fiedler cites are more problematical candidates. Only if we expand our notion of the Faust myth to include everyone who is of the Devil's party (or, in purely secular terms, everyone who has flouted society's concept of right and wrong) can we fit Hester Prynne and Huck Finn on to this Procrustean bed.

Of the major characters in *The Scarlet Letter,* Chillingworth most resembles the mad scientist who sells his soul to the Devil. Yet, in terms of his role in Hawthorne's novel, he is *already* damned, perhaps even the Devil himself. Dimmesdale does experience a fall, though it is one that occurs before the novel even begins. Like Faustus, Dimmesdale is plagued by excessive pride; but unlike the diabolic doctor, he repents and chooses salvation in the end. Although Hester remains unrepentent, and even tells Pearl that the scarlet letter is the Devil's mark on her, she—like Dimmesdale—has fallen for passion rather than for knowledge. Hester may believe herself damned for her sin, but Hawthorne does everything he can to convince the reader otherwise. The true guilt of Hester and Dimmesdale lies not in their fornication (Chillingworth's obvious impotence renders them technically innocent of the more serious charge of adultery), but in their prolonged separation from each other, their mutual violation of "the sanctity of a human heart." By the end of the novel both characters have repented of this transgression, and both are "saved." At worst, Hester is a Faust *manqué.*

The same is even more true of Huck Finn. He may be deadly earnest in his resolve to "go to Hell," but his Mephistopheles is nothing more sinister than his memory of Jim's loyalty and kindness. Also, like Hester and Dimmesdale, Huck "falls" for passion (or compassion) rather than knowledge. Finally, if Hawthorne was Puritan enough to think fornication a sin, Twain was not Confederate enough to think the same of freeing a slave. Unlike Hester and

Dimmesdale, Huck has never done violence to the sanctity of the heart. In order for the Faust myth to work, one must believe (or at least suspend disbelief) in both the reality and justice of Faust's damnation. The audience of *The Scarlet Letter* and *Huckleberry Finn* can do neither.

The fact that one can raise objections to certain of Fiedler's arguments is not a fatal flaw of *Love and Death in the American Novel*. Whether or not we agree with him, Fiedler makes it impossible for us ever to read the classic novels of our literature in the same way again. To be sure, his work would be less vulnerable to attack if it contained fewer factual errors and was more scrupulous in acknowledging the specific influence of other scholars. And yet, what Fiedler does wrong is ultimately less outrageous than what he does right. A fall 1967 review of the revised edition of *Love and Death* may have characterized his achievement best in saying: "What is most important . . . is that here at last is a critical work compatible with the style and tone of the works it purports to discuss, a breakthrough in the last stronghold of WASP 'good taste'—the criticism of our own great untidy, unruly, but mythically potent fiction."[6] The author of this "review" was Leslie Fiedler.

## Chapter Six
# The American Other

Leslie Fiedler's approach to literary anthropology is perhaps best summarized by his statement: "I'm more interested in defining what's human by the marginal than by the central."[1] At its most extreme, this philosophy has led to Fiedler's fascination with such exotica as extraterrestrial fantasies and circus freaks. In his slightly more conventional studies of American culture he has been concerned with those people traditionally excluded from the mainstream of society, principally our two most prominent colored minorities—blacks and Indians. This concern first became evident in "Come Back to the Raft Ag'in, Huck Honey!," was developed at even greater length in *Love and Death in the American Novel,* and has been echoed in numerous books and essays. However, Fiedler's most comprehensive treatments of the American other can be found in *The Return of the Vanishing American* (1968) and the concluding section of *What Was Literature?* (1982).

## Paleface and Redskin

Toward the end of the sixties Fiedler noticed that the Indian, who was a considerably more invisible part of our national life than Ralph Ellison's Negro, was beginning to appear with astonishing frequency in highbrow American literature. Among the writers he mentions are John Barth, Thomas Berger, Ken Kesey, David Markson, Peter Matthiessen, James Leo Herlihy, Leonard Cohen, and "the inspired script writers of *Cat Ballou*" (*R,* 14). These artists (and Fiedler in his own fiction) have "been involved in a common venture: the creation of the New Western, a form which not so much redeems the Pop Western as exploits it with irreverence and pleasure, in contempt of the 'serious reader' and his expectations" (*R,* 14). Before discussing the present situation, however, Fiedler examines the myth of the West as it has developed in the imagination of Europeans and Americans alike.

As we have already seen from his comments on the topological subgenres of the American novel, Fiedler regards the encounter of the white man with the Indian as the defining characteristic of the Western. What we are sometimes apt to forget is that this encounter was dreamed in literature before it occurred in fact. Before Columbus discovered the West, it was assumed that we lived in a tripartite world and that the region beyond the western boundary of that world was inhabited by menacing nonhuman creatures. Over a century after Columbus, as the first reports of the settlement of Jamestown were reaching England, Shakespeare wrote his American fable *The Tempest*. As Fiedler had argued earlier, the image of Caliban represents a typically European view of all Americans. In *The Tempest*, however, Caliban was Shakespeare's nightmare vision only of native Americans—part Moor, part Brazilian-Patagonian-Bermudan Indian, part fish. Moreover, the unspeakable crime attributed to this creature was not cannibalism (as practiced by African savages), but the desire to rape white European women (as represented by Miranda).

After America itself began to be settled, four myths arose that collectively have created our image of the Far West. These are "The Myth of Love in the Woods," or the story of Pocahontas and Captain John Smith; "The Myth of the White Woman with a Tomahawk," which is based on the experience of Hannah Duston, a New England woman who was captured by Indians and fought her way to freedom; "The Myth of the Good Companions in the Woods," the Paleface/Redskin version of the Huck-honey motif, derived from the youthful friendship of fur trader Alexander Henry and the Indian Wawatam; and "The Myth of the Runaway Male," first imagined by Washington Irving in "Rip Van Winkle."

Beginning with the last of these four myths, Fiedler duly acknowledges that the Rip Van Winkle prototype goes back many centuries in German legend, but argues that a distinctively American element was added to the story in Irving's retelling. This is the battle of the sexes, a conflict that Fiedler contends is the American equivalent of the class struggle in European culture. Although Irving's story is set in New York, it is mythologically less a northern than a western story. Rip's antagonist is not the climate or the land, but petticoat government (indeed, it was Irving who invented that marvellously evocative term). By fleeing from the hearth into the wilderness, Rip becomes the comic version of the womanless American hero. In effect, Irving has taken the Teutonic legend of the

Enchanted Sleeper and, by adding a shrewish wife, turned it into "a comic inversion of the legend of the Persecuted Maiden—a corresponding male fantasy of persecution, appropriate to a country that likes to think of itself, or endures being thought of, as the first matriarchy of the modern world" (*R,* 56).

But neither the escape from petticoat government nor the flight into the wilderness are themselves sufficient to make what Fiedler would consider a complete Western. "What makes the Rip myth finally eccentric—and just a little irrelevant—is Irving's failure to dream for Rip appropriate good companions to whom he can flee" (*R,* 59). It remains for Cooper to complete the Western myth by providing Natty Bumppo such a companion in the form of Chingachgook. If one suspects that Fiedler is engaging in special pleading on behalf of the Huck-honey motif, it is only necessary to consider the fate of the Rip story when it was transferred to the stage by Joseph Jefferson. In the melodramatic version of his tale, Rip returns not to a dead but to a chastened wife. Instead of a profound depiction of the misogynist myth, we simply have *Pamela* with the sex roles reversed—the shrew is not defeated, only converted. A good companion in the woods would have provided Dame with stiffer competition.

If Rip Van Winkle belongs to the literature of masculine protest, then Pocahontas—as she is recreated by Captain John Smith—seems more at home as a red-skinned goddess of the sentimental love religion. However, her willingness to sacrifice herself redeems not the alien lover, but her own father. This is because the white sensibility that has created the story begins by defining the Indian as a savage in need of salvation. Thus, Pocahontas betrays her own people out of love for the paleface (in another part of the legend, she slips away from camp to warn the white community of impending attack). Although Fiedler does not make this point, it seems that the Pocahontas myth is roughly equivalent to half the Romeo and Juliet story (Smith, after all, is placed in no danger by his love for the enemy maiden). However, the comic and sentimental nature of this version of the story has made Pocahontas a sort of high-camp icon of the mod Western.

Hannah Duston is an icon very different from Pocahontas (with his flair for schematics Fiedler refers to her as the anti-Pocahontas). According to the story, Mrs. Duston was captured by the Indians when her wimpish husband absconded with seven of their eight

children, leaving her and an infant to fend for themselves (the
Indians, of course, bashed the infant's brains out against a tree, as
Cooper would have his bad savages do in *The Last of the Mohicans*).
Not only did this intrepid lady eventually escape from her captors,
but she took a bounty of scalps with her as well. If Pocahontas
represents the possibility of interracial love, Hannah Duston embodies the reality of interracial strife. Although such strife was the
norm in white-Indian relations, Mrs. Duston's identity as a female
makes her a special case.

In the American version of the Rip Van Winkle myth, we have
seen a dominant wife and a passive husband; however, in the Hannah
Duston story the wife becomes a heroine rather than a comic butt.
Fiedler describes the statue of Hannah Duston in Haverhill, Massachusetts, as "the stone figure of a longskirted, sunbonneted woman
with a tomahawk raised aloft in her delicate hand—so like the
standard Freudian dream of the castrating mother that it is hard to
believe it has not been torn down long since by some maimed New
England male just out of analysis" (*R,* 91).

As we have noted, "The Myth of the Good Companions in the
Woods" is a variation on the central thesis of "Come Back to the
Raft Ag'in, Huck Honey!"; however, it acquires considerable resonance by being juxtaposed to the other Western myths. The friendship of paleface Alexander Henry and redskin Wawatam, originally
chronicled in Henry's *Adventures* and preserved for high literature
in Thoreau's *A Week on the Concord and Merrimack Rivers,* is obviously
antithetical to the "Woman with the Tomahawk." Not only does
Henry's experience give us an image of interracial love, but it is
one that is achieved in the wilderness in flight from petticoat government (in contrast, Mrs. Duston brings petticoat government *into*
the wilderness). Moreover, Wawatam is different from Pocahontas
because his gender removes the threat of miscegenation and do-
mesticity;[2] and his relationship with Henry makes the European
into a quasi-Indian, whereas that of Pocahontas with John Smith
makes the Indian into a quasi-European.

Although the bonding of Alexander Henry and Wawatam is the
real-life paradigm for an enduring motif in American fiction, few
writers since Cooper have actually made the colored anti-wife an
Indian. (Fiedler suspects that Cooper may have doomed the genre
that he helped to create by portraying his Indians elegiacally, as the
last of a dying breed.) What we have instead are crypto-Indians

disguised as members of other races—Melville's Queequeg as a South Sea islander, Twain's Jim as a runaway slave (Twain's practice is explained by his genocidal hatred of real Indians). Consequently, attempts to redeem the Western for high literature have tended to be problematic. Fiedler demonstrates that Poe's one venture in this genre—*The Journal of Julius Rodman*—is "a hopeless jumbling together of the Southern and the Western, to the detriment of both" (*R*, 129); and that Walter Van Tilburg Clark's moving novel *The Oxbow Incident* (whose chief villain is an ex-Confederate general and most important colored man a Negro) is finally not a Western "but an anti-Southern in a Western landscape . . . an illustrated sermon *against* lynching" (*R*, 142).

When the Western once again became an acceptable genre in high literature, the tone had become irreverent and debunking. Fiedler sees the roots of the "New Western" in Hemingway's first published novel. A farce about Indian life masquerading as a parody of Sherwood Anderson, *The Torrents of Spring* exploits "the clichés and stereotypes of all the popular books which precede it . . . , bringing the full weight of their accumulated absurdities to bear in every casual quip" (*R*, 147). The next notable attempt to make the Western into self-conscious camp can be found in Nathanael West's satirical depiction of a drugstore cowboy and a Yiddish Indian in *The Day of the Locust*. For reasons that seem to baffle Fiedler, this inchoate genre did not reach fruition until 1960 when John Barth's *The Sot-Weed Factor* (a burlesque of the Pocahontas myth) gave rise to a whole spate of New Westerns, which produced neither a new myth nor an antimyth, but rather an antistereotype.

If there is a major weakness in *The Return of the Vanishing American*, it is in the brevity of Fiedler's discussion of specific New Western texts. His delineation of the various Western myths is so fascinating and suggestive that one expects a full-scale application of those myths to the relevant literature (maybe not on the order of *Love and Death in the American Novel*, but certainly more than he gives us). Thomas Berger's *Little Big Man* is itself a treasure trove that would reward detailed analysis. (The hint of fabulation in Jack Crabb's point of view—combining the ambiguity of Young Goodman Brown and the wish-fulfillment of Walter Mitty—along with the novel's pseudoscholarly narrative frame turns *Little Big Man* into a metahistorical tale.) Now that film versions have been made of three of the novels that Fiedler mentions (*Little Big Man, Midnight Cowboy,* and *One Flew Over the Cuckoo's Nest*) and the Indian has come into his own as author as well as character (M. Scott Momaday and James Welch to name only the two most obvious figures), the time may be right for a second *Return of the Vanishing American*.

## Life Among the Lowly

As Fiedler's own aesthetic tastes grew more egalitarian, he became increasingly interested in opening up the canon of accepted literature. Thus, he began to ask himself what differentiated the American novels admired by academics from such an enduring popular favorite as Harriet Beecher Stowe's *Uncle Tom's Cabin*. What he discovered was that the so-called classic novels "were not only more elegantly structured and textured, more ideologically dense, more overtly subversive—more difficult and challenging, in short—but they almost invariably celebrated the flight from civilization and the settlement, church and school, from everything which had survived (under female auspices) of Christian humanism in the New World— thus reinforcing the myth of Home as Hell" (*WWL*, 151–52). Having spent the bulk of his career discussing such books, Fiedler finally turns his attention—in *What Was Literature?*—to the largely female countertradition that celebrates Home as Heaven.

Because the reconciliation implicit in interracial male bonding is central to the wilderness myth as Fiedler has long defined it, it is only fitting that the horror of miscegenation (more especially interethnic rape) be a key element of the domestic myth. And, sure enough, Fiedler finds a series of narratives that exemplify his thesis. This series begins with *Uncle Tom's Cabin* itself (along with the various "Tom plays" into which it was translated), and continues with Thomas Dixon, Jr.'s *The Leopard's Spots* and *The Clansman* (and preeminently their more famous adaptation as D. W. Griffith's *The Birth of a Nation*), Margaret Mitchell's *Gone With the Wind* (as both novel and movie), and Alex Haley's *Roots* (from *Reader's Digest* condensation through best-selling book to television miniseries). "Read as a single work composed over more than a century, in many media and by many hands," Fiedler argues, "these constitute a hitherto unperceived 'epic,' embodying a myth of our history unequaled in scope and resonance by any work of High Art" (*WWL*, 154). Although this rather sweeping evaluation is open to question, the theory of the "inadvertent epic" helps to illuminate an intriguing dialogue in American popular culture.

Those who have read *Love and Death in the American Novel* will recognize several of the motifs that Fiedler finds in *Uncle Tom's Cabin* as coming straight from the sentimental love religion discussed in that earlier critical tome. To begin with, the Protestant feminization of Christ is everywhere in Mrs. Stowe's novel. The moral exemplars in *Uncle Tom's Cabin* are almost all women, many of them mothers. Even when we have a bad mother in the person of Marie St. Clare (prototype for a whole succession of spoiled Southern belles, most notably Faulkner's egregious Mrs. Compson), surrogate mothers rush in to fill the void: there is the prim and righteous Miss Ophelia and Little Eva's warmhearted Mammy, not to mention Eva herself, who is something of a mother to both her father and the devilish Topsy (as Fiedler has suggested in *Love and Death,* Eva and Topsy are a pint-sized contrast of snow maiden and dark lady). There is also the memory of St. Clare's dead mother (who, appropriately, bears the same name as his daughter), a memory that sustains Augustine (named for the saint who was converted by his mother) as he is himself on his deathbed. But perhaps the most important avatar of the maternal Christ is Uncle Tom himself.

Militant blacks are technically correct in asserting that Uncle Tom is a passive figure who has been robbed of his masculinity (a case made most forcefully by James Baldwin in his anti-Tom essay "Everybody's Protest Novel"). What they neglect to note (or simply dismiss as irrelevant) is the fact that Mrs. Stowe regards Tom's Christ-like suffering as a sign of his moral superiority. The Christ who exhorted his followers to turn the other cheek was arguing for virtues traditionally associated with femininity. Mrs. Stowe saw Negroes as being "naturally patient, timid, and unenterprising." Because they were "home-loving and affectionate,"[3] she considered them an essentially feminine, and hence Christ-like, people. Although these views may be judged racist and sexist according to "enlightened" modern standards, they are perfectly consistent with the bourgeois Protestant piety that has helped shape the novel since the time of Samuel Richardson.

What is most significant about *Uncle Tom's Cabin* and the other narratives in Fiedler's inadvertent epic is not their ideology or theology, but their ability to create characters and scenes of truly mythic proportions, "primordial images . . . [that] emerge mysteriously from the collective unconscious and pass, scarcely mediated by [an] almost transparent text, into the public domain, to which, like all authentic popular literature, they properly belong" (*WWL,* 161). In this regard, it is significant to note that all of the works in the inadvertent epic began as novels but reached their widest audience in the form of popular drama. For Thomas Dixon, Jr.'s anti-Tom polemics this transformation occurred in the first great film of the American cinema, D. W. Griffith's *The Birth of a Nation.*

In *Uncle Tom's Cabin* the all-important theme of interethnic rape is present exclusively in the violation of black slave women by their white masters. One even suspects that Mrs. Stowe's strongest objection to slavery was that it offended Puritan notions of sexual propriety. (The only character in her novel to manifest overt sexual desire is the diabolical slave owner Simon Legree.) In writing his defense of the South a half century later, Dixon maintains Stowe's reverence for the home and her revulsion at the thought of interethnic rape. He has simply reversed the racial roles, giving us the nightmare image of the black satyr aflame to ravish the Confederate snow maiden. The fact that sociologists will tell us that this image is primarily a Freudian projection of the guilt felt by white Southerners for the sort of prurience that Mrs. Stowe describes in no way dissipates the mythic power of the nightmare itself.

In one sense the American Civil War can be viewed as a battle of the books. Abraham Lincoln was convinced that the conflict was started by Harriet Beecher Stowe, and Mark Twain was just as certain that the culprit was Sir Walter Scott. Rather than diminishing Scott's influence on the South, the Confederate defeat simply enhanced the desire for romantic self-delusion. Dixon quite explicitly equates the Ku Klux Klan with the heroic highlanders of the Waverley novels. The image of these white knights on horseback, dreamed by Dixon and filmed by Griffith, "has provided the model for a million B-movie rides to the rescue, in which, no matter how stereotyped, it never quite loses its primordial power" (*WWL,* 194).

That this primordial power ultimately transcends boundaries of ideology and culture is attested to by Fiedler's own observation. He tells us that "I myself once saw . . . the members of a left-wing ciné club in Athens, believers all in the equality of the races and the unmitigated evil of the Klan, rise to their feet at ten o'clock in the morning (the year was 1960, two wars and innumerable revolutions after the making of the film) to scream with bloodlust and approval equal to that of the racist first-nighters of 1915 as white womanhood was once more delivered from the threat of black rape" (*WWL,* 194).

Margaret Mitchell's contribution to the inadvertent epic was "the feminization of the anti-Tom novel." Like Stowe, Dixon, and Griffith before her, she valued the domestic life as the locus of meaning and order in an otherwise threatening cosmos. Of the four characters whom she has contributed to our popular mythos, the sole black (Mammy) comes closest to being a moral norm. Along with Mrs. Stowe, Margaret Mitchell shares the patronizing view of blacks as essentially maternal people who rarely aspire to a life beyond the confines of home and hearth. With Dixon, she feels that blacks are happiest within a hierarchical social order in which they are not encouraged by carpetbaggers and abolitionists to seek elevation from their proper station in life. The black maid in *The Birth of a Nation* who identifies with the South and scorns "free niggers" and "white trash" is a blatant precursor of Mammy. Although a generally passive figure, Uncle Tom is fundamentally different in that his loyalty is to Christianity rather than to the Confederacy. The one thing that Simon Legree can never get him to do is to violate his conscience by beating the other slaves.

Despite the obvious resemblances between *Gone With the Wind* and the other narratives that Fiedler discusses, Mitchell's novel does not seem sufficiently concerned with interethnic rape to fit the pattern of the inadvertent epic. Although Scarlett O'Hara comes close to being raped by a black during Reconstruction and is properly avenged by the Klan, that scene is not at the mythic center of the novel. Two other sexual encounters are. In the first of these Scarlett experiences a kind of erotic ecstasy when she guns down a would-be Yankee attacker (the first-night crowd in Atlanta went wild). In the second, an inebriated Rhett Butler takes her by force and presumably makes a woman of the coquettish belle. What is most memorable about *Gone With the Wind* is not so much its images of race as its story of intraethnic sex. The three white characters who have made it into the realm of myth (Scarlett, Rhett, and Ashley) constitute an archetypal love triangle.[4] The ineffectually Apollonian Ashley and the vitally Dionysian Rhett are actually male counterparts of the snow maiden and the dark lady, with Scarlett—a combination Pamela and Lovelace—masquerading as Clarissa.

With Alex Haley's *Roots* we have a book that is squarely in the tradition defined by Stowe and Dixon. Indeed, Fiedler seems to regard Haley's moving potboiler as a kind of dialectical synthesis created by the clash of Stowe's thesis and Dixon's antithesis. What distinguishes *Roots* from the other parts of the inadvertent epic is that it is created by a black artist. Fiedler's explanation why it has taken so long for a black to reach the majority audience with a story as mythically potent as those of Stowe, Dixon, and Mitchell is simple but persuasive. Out of a sense of racial assertiveness, black writers such as Richard Wright have accepted and glorified the image of the bad (i.e., "uppity") "nigger" projected by Dixon. When black rape is justified on sociological grounds, as in Wright's *Native Son;* or on historical grounds, as in William Styron's *The Confessions of Nat Turner;*[5] or on political grounds, as in Eldridge Cleaver's *Soul on Ice;* it may go over with the radical chic crowd, but is not likely to play in Peoria. What is needed is an epic with a broad enough appeal to enthrall a biracial middle-class audience.

What Haley has done is to write a socially conservative tale based loosely on the experience of his mother's family. The Gambian society from which his ancestor Kunta Kinte was stolen comes across as an African version of middle America—more Beaver Cleaver than Eldridge Cleaver (Kunta's dedication to learning and self-improvement reads like an ad for the United Negro College Fund). When transplanted to America, Kunta dreams of freedom but finally settles down to a conventionally patriarchal home life. His descendants all harbor bourgeois values and advance themselves through determination and hard work. We are told, on the back-cover blurb of the paperback edition of *Roots,* that the saga "ends . . . at the funeral of a black professor whose children are a teacher, a Navy architect, an assistant director of the U.S. Information Agency, and an author. The author is Alex Haley."

Because the middle-class roots of Kunta Kinte's family are posited as African, Haley can make his characters "good niggers" without seeming to capitulate to the dominant white culture. Haley also makes a play for the black militant audience by emphasizing Kunta's Moslem faith. (Because that faith is inherited rather than chosen, the white audience is not alienated by an explicit rejection of Christianity.) Also, there is sufficient interethnic rape and flagellation (exclusively white on black) to appeal consciously to the righteous indignation of all but the most rabid racist and subconsciously to the prurience of all but the most confirmed ascetic. As a veteran of the U.S. Coast Guard and *Reader's Digest* and the ghost author of *The Autobiography of Malcolm X,* Haley knows how to play both ends against the middle. In Kunta Kinte, he has created a brilliant synthesis of Uncle Tom and Malcolm X. As Nigger Jim (no doubt another of Haley's ancestors) once said: "It's too good to be true, Honey. It's too good to be true."

## For Sam and Hattie

The final section of *What Was Literature?* completes the foray into literary anthropology that Fiedler had begun over three decades earlier with "Come Back to the Raft Ag'in, Huck Honey!" By exploring the feminine, domestic myth of America (complete with its idealization of the hearth and its obsessive fear of miscegenetic rape), Fiedler is not so much repudiating the misogynist tradition of interethnic male bonding that he has long argued lies at the heart of our most essential fiction as expanding the canon to include that countervision to which the Huck-honey motif stands in dialectical tension.

It is perhaps fitting that during their later years, Samuel Clemens and Harriet Beecher Stowe lived next door to each other in Hartford, Connecticut, equally rich and famous—she for "celebrating Home and Mother," he "for fantasizing escapes from both" (*WWL,* 242). In the concluding chapter to *What Was Literature?,* Fiedler tries to put our fractured literary heritage back together by contending that both these grand figures are worthy of homage ("if Sam Clemens is a literary father to us all, Hattie Stowe is our mother" [*WWL,* 243]), and even goes so far as to dedicate the book to "Sam and Hattie." Finally, he suggests that, at certain levels, there are surprising links between the presumably antithetical world views of our literary parents. It is, however, an argument that even Fiedler concedes works better for Clemens than for Stowe. All that really connects Hattie to Sam is the fact that her "characters travel the Mississippi and its tributaries, not merely in quest of a home but in flight from enemies rather like those who beset Huck and Jim" (*WWL,* 240).

All of his life Sam Clemens was a mama's boy whose rebellion against home was the ambivalent charade of a Tom Sawyer, and his many descriptions of domestic life—particularly of the Phelps farm, based on the home of his uncle John A. Quarles—contain an undercurrent of affection beneath the surface irony. At the end of his life, with his wife and daughters dead, Clemens was a lost and pathetic figure:

Hair white, mustache white, clothes white, he must have seemed not, as he liked to boast, the "only clean man in a dirty world," but a ghost reenacting the macho ritual of the mining camp and the saloon, with no woman left to say him nay. All alone, he would smoke, we are told, forty cigars a day, drink God knows how many shots of bourbon, and end playing pool with himself, until he passed out on the billiard table and was carried off to bed by a servant. There doubtless, in intervals between the nightmares of diminution and dissolution recorded in his last unfinished sketches, he must surely have had good dreams, too. But it is hard to say whether he dreamed himself in them as imposter, warmly embraced by Aunt Sally as her own dear sister's son, or a kinless boy forever in flight with an eternally fugitive slave. (*WWL,* 245)

# Chapter Seven
# Next Year in Jerusalem

During the fifties and sixties one of the most notable developments in American literature was the appearance of a large number of talented Jewish writers. Like the so-called Southern Renaissance of a generation earlier, this phenomenon has been attributed to the social transition caused by the assimilation of an insular and traditional subculture into the mainstream of American life. Such upheaval creates the sort of introspection that produces a wide variety of literary effects—from broad comedy to high tragedy. As a critic Fiedler has observed the rise and eventual demise of this Jewish Renaissance. As a Jew who remains proud of his cultural heritage, he has been a participant as well as an observer. Perhaps for this reason the otherwise acerbic Grant Webster concedes that "In his more sober and scholarly moments Fiedler has traced and documented the entry of the Jew into our national literary culture better than anyone else. . . . Almost despite himself he is kind of an American Moses leading the Jewish intellectual community—his people—to the promised land of the republic of letters."[1]

## The Lost Tribes of Israel

In the introduction to his 1971 collection of essays *To the Gentiles,* Fiedler says that the thesis of "Master of Dreams: The Jew in a Gentile World" is "as near as I suspect I ever shall [come] to a final mythical definition of the situation which defines me as well as many of the writers whom I most love" *(CE,* 2:3). Beginning with the biblical story of Joseph, Fiedler argues that the primary archetypal role that the Jew has imagined for himself in a predominantly non-Jewish culture has been that of the dream merchant. The point is made explicitly in the sixth satire of that *goyish* poet Juvenal, where in the midst of an inventory of all of the tempting goods on sale in Rome, he tells us that " 'for a few pennies' one can buy any dream his heart desires 'from the Jews' " *(CE,* 2:176). Since Joseph experienced both persecution and success because of his dreams (and

71

his ability to interpret the dreams of others), his story is broad enough to explain the peculiar position that Jews have traditionally occupied in the Western, Gentile world.

Fiedler does make a strategic qualification when he admits that the image of dream master is more often a Jewish self-perception than a Gentile stereotype. "When the Gentile dreams the Jew in his midst, . . . he dreams him as the vengeful and villainous Father: Shylock or Fagin, the Bearded Terror threatening some poor full-grown *goy* with a knife, or inducting some guileless Gentile kid into a life of crime." This is because "Shylock and Fagin are shadows cast upon the Christian world by that first Jewish Father, Abraham, who is to them circumcizer and sacrificer rolled into one—castrator, in short" (*CE,* 2:177). The Jewish imagination, however, always sees Abraham releasing his son, after the moment of intended sacrifice. In turn that son, Isaac, becomes the father of Jacob who is the father of Joseph. Although Joseph himself had offspring, he lives in the mythic memory not as another father, but as the favorite son who makes good and thus provides salvation for both the Gentiles and his own family. That this schematic description can also be applied to Jesus (who for Christians is the salvific favored son of God) suggests why the biblical Joseph is so important to the Jewish imagination and why he is a luxury that the Gentile mind (insofar as it is shaped by Christian myth) cannot afford.

Although Fiedler claims that his archetypal formulation holds up for the entire history of Jewish/Gentile relations, he is specifically concerned with the literary Jew in the modern world. For our time the role of Joseph the dreamer has been divided into the two figures of physician and artist—specifically Sigmund Freud and Franz Kafka, "which is to say, the Healer and the Patient he could not have healed, since he is another, an alternative version of himself " (*CE,* 2:178). As doctor and scientist, Freud represents the rational mind wrestling with the forces of the unconscious, which are largely the product of our conflicts with our parents. In his masterwork *The Interpretation of Dreams* "obsession is turned into vision, guilt into knowledge, *trauma* into *logos.*" As victim and seer, Kafka represents the power of the imagination to apprehend that which cannot be understood, to confront that which cannot be overcome. "Between them, Kafka and Freud, the crippled poet and the triumphant savant . . . have helped to determine the shape of Jewish-American writing in the first half of the twentieth century" (*CE,* 2:182).

Although Fiedler's ensuing discussion mentions the work of Delmore Schwartz, Allen Ginsberg, and Henry Roth, the primary focus of attention is on Nathanael West's *The Dream Life of Balso Snell* and Norman Mailer's *An American Dream.* West's novel is a highly surrealistic account of a tour through Western civilization as it is preserved inside the Trojan horse. It is significant that the vehicle of culture is Greek and that the Jewish protagonist can enter it only through the anus. "Not for him, the High Road to Culture *via* the 'horse's mouth,' nor the mystical way of 'contemplating the naval'; only the 'Acherontic' Freudian back entrance: the anal-sexual approach. 'Tradesmen enter by the rear' " (*CE,* 2:183). For all of its sophomoric obscurity and vulgarity, *Balso Snell* is significant for being an apprentice work that introduces some of the themes that West would develop more skillfully in his three remaining novels. It is also the most explicit declaration of Jewishness in West's fiction and his one work most obviously influenced by Kafka.

The narrative line of Mailer's novel is considerably easier to follow; however, it too deviates from realism. If West's Balso Snell is an American Kafka, Mailer's Stephen Rojack more nearly resembles a hip Freud. Rojack is a former congressman, a television personality, and a professor of "existential psychology." Not only has he won public respect and adulation, but he also fulfills his private fantasies. This involves doing battle with three shikses who represent various aspects of Potiphar's wife. His own wife is an arrogant upper-class bitch whom he murders in a fit of rage. Before disposing of the body, he finds time for a quick tryst with the German maid, whom he enters from the same orifice that took Balso Snell inside the Trojan horse. His last conquest is of a blond girl with the suggestive name of Cherry. Before he can totally possess her, however, he must fight off a black man who threatens him with a knife. The macho Jew defeats the "spade," but finds his victory to be Pyrrhic when the enraged friends of his assailant murder the golden girl in revenge. The novel closes with Rojack's making a phone call to Cherry in Heaven. At this point, she evokes the image of the ultimate dream shikse and cinematic sex goddess by telling him that "Marilyn says to say hello."

Although Judaism is more readily identifiable as a religion than as a race or culture (strictly speaking, it is neither of the latter two), we tend to associate modern Jews more with their secular achievements than with their religious piety. Thus, it seems hardly remarkable that Simone Weil was born into a family of prosperous agnostic Jews. Nor is it surprising that during her early years she was committed to a rather conventional variety of Marxist socialism. What makes her a memorable, even a scandalous, figure is her transformation into a Christian ascetic who has become the object of a cult among Catholic existentialists. Fiedler's own role in introducing her work to the American public, through a long article in the January 1951 issue of *Commentary,* won him prominent mention in *Time* and his first taste of national notoriety. He received favorable responses from Herbert Read and Upton Sinclair and "even offers of audiences with the Pope and Sholem Asch, both of which temptations I managed finally to resist; in short, distinguished recognition and some comic relief." Moreover, Fiedler has been told that "at the same moment that a doctor in the Celebes was sitting down to write me a note of appreciation, a professor in the Hebrew University . . . was hurling the *Commentary* containing my article through a window" (*CE,* 2:32).

Simone Weil (who died in 1943 at the age of thirty-four) manages to generate such passionate feelings because of the extremity of her life and thought. When she was five, she refused to eat sugar as long as it remained unavailable to the soldiers at the front. Later on, she went without socks because the children of the workers could not afford them. As a young adult she worked as a teacher, "joining the workers in their sports, marching with them in their picket lines, taking part with the unemployed in their pick and shovel work, and refusing to eat more than the rations of those on relief, distributing her surplus food to the needy" (*CE,* 2:15−16).

When these gestures failed to get her teaching license revoked, Simone Weil simply quit her post and joined the class struggle fulltime by becoming a worker at the Renault auto plant. This lasted until her health gave out. What followed was a short period of rest, after which she set off for Spain to support the Loyalists, vowing never to use the gun that she was issued. In a ridiculously anticlimactic accident she was injured by boiling oil and taken by her parents to recuperate in Portugal. It was here that she had the epiphany crucial to her conversion. When listening to a Gregorian chant at a time when her migraine was at its worst, she experienced a sense of Christ's passion. Shortly thereafter, she met a young English Catholic who introduced her to the work of the British metaphysical poets. In particular, George Herbert's poem "Love bade me welcome" took on for her the significance of a prayer.

Although her movement toward Christianity was sufficient to evoke hysteria among those who were bereft of any faith other than a kind of liberal hostility toward faith itself, Simone Weil died before deciding to be baptized or making any gesture toward formal affiliation with a church. She saw herself as the ultimate outsider whose particular martyrdom lay in remaining forever "at the intersection of Christianity and everything that is not Christianity" (see *CE*, 2:9). Her Catholic friends, and many readers who never knew her, are convinced that had she lived, Weil would have entered the church and perhaps even have been canonized. As it is, she remains an unofficial saint for our time, speaking "of the problems of belief in the vocabulary of the unbeliever" (*CE*, 2:5). Because she wrote as well as lived her faith, she continues to witness for it from beyond the grave. The nature of her legacy is best summed up by Fiedler when he writes:

As the life of Simone Weil reflects a desire to insist on the absolute even at the risk of being absurd, so her writing tends always toward the extreme statement, the formulation that shocks by its willingness to push to its ultimate conclusion the kind of statement we ordinarily accept with the tacit understanding that no one will take it *too* seriously. The outrageous (from the natural point of view) ethics of Christianity, the paradoxes on which it is based, are a scandal to common sense; but we have protected ourselves against them by turning them imperceptibly into platitudes. It is Simone Weil's method to revivify them, by re-creating them in all their pristine offensiveness. (*CE*, 2:23–24)

By the early 1980s the conflict between blacks and Jews was so apparent that the indiscreet remarks of Jesse Jackson and Louis Farrakhan and the more genteel ethnocentricity of Ed Koch and Meir Kahane struck us less as a revelation of unsuspected prejudice than as a breach of accepted political hypocrisy. In the mid-1950s, however, "Rastas" and "Hymie" were considered the best of friends because of their joint exclusion from polite society (there were signs along stretches of Miami Beach that prohibited "Negroes, Jews, and dogs"). At that time, only prescient types such as James Baldwin and Leslie Fiedler could see the coming rift. It is therefore fitting that Fiedler's earliest statement on this issue—"Negro and Jew:

Encounter in America"—should be a review-essay inspired by Baldwin's *Notes of a Native Son.*

The most obvious difference between Negro and Jew (as they were then known) is their relationship to America. Jews were late refugees who fled persecution in Europe to find opportunity and tolerance (if not acceptance) in the New World. The Jew, at least, prior to his assimilation, represented Europe to America. The Negro, on the other hand, has been in America since its very beginning and remains a living reminder of our failure to live up to our professed ideals. As such, he represents—figuratively as well as literally—the dark face of America to the rest of the world.

At a deeper, mythological, level, the Jew is neither white nor black, but a third race. He is Shem, the son of Noah, trying at various times to pass as his black brother Ham or his white brother Japheth. To the extent that he is discriminated against by Japheth, Shem is allied with Ham; however, when he seeks to assimilate himself into Japheth's culture, it is frequently by baiting Ham. As Fiedler was perceptive enough to note in the mid-sixties, even the liberal Jew would eventually see his faith in human equality challenged by the intractable reality of black failure. Before affirmative action became a national policy, Fiedler could see that blacks would ultimately need to demand "*special privilege* rather than equality if they are to make it at all in the very world in which the Jews have so preeminently flourished" (*CE*, 2:171).

Black anti-Semitism derives from a variety of sources. Among lower-class blacks it tends to be a variation of that strain of white populism that sees the Jew as the prototypical capitalist exploiter. The most visible embodiment of this image for most poor blacks is the Jewish shopkeeper, who is physically located in the ghetto (a term borrowed from the experience of European Jewry) but who exists sociologically in that no-man's-land between Ham and Japheth. Insofar as he is religious, or is imagined to be such, the Jew is an affront to both the black Christian and the black Muslim. The former perceives the Jews as having both crucified Christ and heckled Simon of Cyrene when he helped carry the cross. The latter are "obsessed by the legendary notion of the 'Evil Jacob,' Israel the Usurper—as well as the myth of Isaac before him doing poor Ishmael out of his heritage" (*CE*, 2:167).

In his response to Baldwin's book, Fiedler provides a personal perspective on the encounter of Negro and Jew by remembering his own experiences with black people. Although none of his best friends is black, he has known a good number of blacks throughout his life. These include maids who have worked for his family, a porter with whom he worked at a shoe store when still in his teens, and fellow members of various radical organizations. His most vivid memory, however, is of walking to school in the ninth grade through a poor black neighborhood. He particularly remembers the disconcerting feeling that he was in hostile territory and that his own belief in racial equality did not render him safe from attack. One day when walking with his mother through this run-down neighborhood, he recalls her pointing "to one of those drab, alien houses from which I had shrunk day after day, saying 'I was born there' " (*CE,* 1:469). This familiar pattern of urban decay, of the Negro moving in when the Jew moves out, suggests that as Ham is to Shem, so is Shem to Japheth. Thus, "no Jew can selflessly dedicate himself to the fight for the equality of the Negro; when he pretends that he is not also fighting for himself, he is pretending that he is indistinguishable from a *goy*" (*CE,* 1:470).

## My Son the Critic

One of Fiedler's most comprehensive Jewish essays (it was actually published as a monograph by the Herzl Press) is "The Jew in the American Novel." Although this is meant to be more of a survey than a theoretical discussion, Fiedler's own tastes help to establish a canon of Jewish-American literature that is somewhat different from the consensus that existed at the time he was writing (1959). In particular, he attempts to rescue such neglected novelists as Abraham Cahan, Daniel Fuchs, and Henry Roth; and to challenge the esteem accorded to such overrated hacks as Ludwig Lewisohn and Ben Hecht.

Although the Jew has appeared as a figure in American fiction since Charles Brockden Brown's *Arthur Mervyn,* he was until the 1930s largely the creation of Gentile writers trying to come to terms with the stranger in their midst (Hemingway's Robert Cohn, for example, is a more compelling character and a more real Jew than any of the creations of Ludwig Lewisohn). Indeed, the first "Jewish-American" novelist was a Gentile named Henry Harland who wrote under the pen name of Sidney Luska. Along with such authentic Jews as Cahan, Lewisohn, and Hecht, Luska wrote a kind of erotic fiction in which the problems of Jewish assimilation to American culture were posed in terms of sexual symbols. This theme, which Fiedler calls "Zion as Eros," would dominate the Jewish novel until replaced by the proletarian consciousness of the thirties.

The American novelists most celebrated in the 1930s were responding to the social crisis posed by the Great Depression. Because of the infatuation of many Jewish intellectuals with communism, it is not surprising that Jews were among the major contributors to the proletarian and Popular Front literature of the period. Moreover, with the urbanization of the American novel begun by the Gentile Theodore Dreiser, the time was right for predominantly city-dwelling Jews to make their mark in American fiction. When we look back at the thirties, however, Jews such as Edward Dahlberg, Leonard Ehrlich, Daniel Fuchs, Meyer Levin, and Mike Gold (the last of whom was called, with some justification, the "Al Jolson of the Communist movement") still seem less prepossessing than Gentiles John Steinbeck, John Dos Passos, and James T. Farrell. In Fiedler's opinion, the two most important Jewish novelists of the thirties were apolitical men largely ignored in their own time— Nathanael West and Henry Roth.

Although a writer of considerable promise whose actual achievement is highly regarded today (more than four decades after his untimely death in 1940), West was a novelist whose Jewishness always seemed marginal. This is no doubt due to the paucity of Jewish characters in his fiction and to his own consciously *goyish* life-style (e.g., wearing Brooks Brothers suits and hunting with Faulkner). And yet, West reads like nothing so much as an American Kafka. "It seems to me inconceivable," Fiedler writes, "that anyone but an urban, second-generation Jew in revolt against his background could have produced the novels from *Balso Snell* to *The Day of the Locust*" (*CE*, 2:95–96). Roth, on the other hand, wrote a specifically Jewish book in his single novel, *Call It Sleep* (1935). Technically influenced by Joycean stream of consciousness, *Call It Sleep* is a sensitive portrayal of two years in the life of a poor Jewish boy named David: "In the place of the Marxian class struggle, Roth sets an almost Dickensian vision of the struggle between the child and society, of the child as Pure Victim" (*CE*, 2:96). Although Fiedler succeeded almost single-handedly in getting *Call It Sleep* republished, Henry Roth never wrote another novel.

As we have previously noted, Jewish assimilation into the mainstream of American society took a quantum leap in the period following World War II. With the end of mass immigration, the Jewish population consisted increasingly of second- and third-generation Americans. At the same time, Hitler had decimated the Jewish population of Europe. Thus, Jews were becoming fully integrated Americans as never before. "No longer is our story that of the rise of an occasional David Levinsky," Fiedler writes, "but that of almost the whole Jewish people on the march towards the suburbs; of the transformation of essential Jewish life into bourgeois life" (*CE,* 2:98).

One of the consequences of this process was the emergence of Jewish literature at all levels of the cultural spectrum. At the lowest level, where overt anti-Semitism still had its strongest hold, the essentially invisible Jerome Siegal and Joe Shuster invented the first great comic book hero, Superman. Also science fiction, the first lower-middlebrow genre to challenge the hegemony of the Western and the detective story, was dominated by Jews. ("The notion of the Jewish cowboy is utterly ridiculous, of a Jewish detective, Scotland Yard variety or private eye, nearly as anomalous; but to think of the scientist as a Jew is almost tautological" [*CE,* 2:102].) It was at the middle and upper reaches of middlebrow culture, however, that Jewish writers gained greatest respectability.

Writers such as Irwin Shaw, Herman Wouk, and Budd Schulberg lacked the philosophical depth, moral subtlety, and technical virtuosity that we associate with the highest art; however, they were literate enough and right-minded enough to be fashionable among upwardly mobile suburbanites. The anti-anti-Semitic novel (by both Jew and Gentile) was a particular rage during the late forties and early fifties. This genre consisted of such pious liberal tracts as Arthur Miller's *Focus,* Laura Z. Hobson's *Gentleman's Agreement,* Mary Jane Ward's *The Professor's Umbrella,* and John Hersey's *The Wall.* Even the post–World War II antiwar novel (e.g., Irwin Shaw's *The Young Lions*) contributed to this trend by introducing the figure of the Jewish Sad Sack who at the crucial moment proves just as macho as his WASP tormenters.

Finally, during the fifties, two middlebrow Jewish writers created representative American prototypes of the period. In Marjorie Morningstar, Herman Wouk made a suburban Jewish housewife into a symbol of bourgeois respectability and interfaith tolerance, while

J. D. Salinger gave us the ultimately sensitive and misunderstood adolescent in Holden Caulfield. Since then Wouk (like the late Irwin Shaw) has graduated to writing television miniseries, and Salinger has disappeared into the mountain fastness of New Hampshire where he can do his Zen meditations behind the protection of barbed wire and guard dogs.

And yet, when critics speak of the Jewish literary renaissance, they are not referring to *Superman* comic books, science fiction, or middlebrow best-sellers, but to the cosmopolitan combination of political commitment and highbrow aesthetics that characterizes contributors to the *Partisan Review*. Although Fiedler appeared frequently in its pages early in his career, his relationship with *Partisan Review* has been stormy. After publishing a sober and balanced analysis of that journal in the spring 1956 issue of *Perspectives, USA,* he received an angry letter from *Partisan*'s editors forbidding him from ever again appearing in its pages (an excommunication that actually lasted three years). He admires the magazine for its willingness to deal with ideas, for its long-time independence from the academy,[2] and for its discovery of certain writers and critics who have since made a lasting contribution to American letters. However, as his own aesthetic principles became more egalitarian, Fiedler grew to distrust the marriage of left-wing politics and literary elitism represented by *Partisan Review*. It seemed not only disingenuous but old-fashioned, the afterglow of a modernist revolution long since fought and won.

Perhaps the most notable contribution that *Partisan Review* has made to Jewish literature in particular and to American culture in general has been in launching the career of Saul Bellow. One of the last great practitioners of the bourgeois, realistic novel, Bellow is vastly (and justly) admired by literary traditionalists. It is to his credit that Fiedler has not allowed changes in critical fashion or his own predilections to alter his high regard for Bellow. What he said of Bellow's style in 1957 still rings true nearly thirty years later: "Muted or released, his language is never dull or merely expedient, but always moves under tension, toward or away from a kind of rich, crazy poetry, a juxtaposition of high and low style, elegance and slang, unlike anything else in English except *Moby Dick,* though at the same time not unrelated in range and variety to spoken Yiddish" (*CE,* 2:63). It is Bellow's peculiar gift to combine this power of language with empathetic insight into the essential loneliness of modern man and the moral ambiguity of his relation to the universe. "Such a man," Fiedler writes, "is at once the Jew in perpetual exile and Huck Finn in whom are blended with perfect irony the twin American beliefs that the answer to all questions is always over the next horizon and that there is no answer now or ever" (*CE*, 2:64).

## Chapter Eight
# Reexamining the Canon

As we have seen, one of Fiedler's most persistent efforts in recent years has been to extend the canon of works accepted as literature. He argues, however, that this does not involve an abandonment, but only a reexamination, of standards. A willingness to take popular literature seriously does not force us to repudiate what has been judged high art, but rather to search for the genuine appeal and value of our great books, not simply taking the word of some pontifical experts as dogma needful for salvation. This was of course the impulse that inspired formalist critics such as John Crowe Ransom to urge a close reading of texts to discover not only the what, but the why and the how of literature we choose to call great. Although his methodology and conclusions are radically different from those of the "close readers," the impulse that motivates Fiedler is essentially similar to theirs.

## Affirming the Void

In the title essay of *No! In Thunder,* Fiedler begins by confessing a dirty secret: that he has always believed the creation and criticism of literature to be moral acts. Since a moralistic approach to literature has long been considered vulgar by the cognoscenti (the sort of thing reserved for high church defenders of culture such as T. S. Eliot or Legion of Decency types), the critic is expected not to deliver homilies, but "to speak of novels and poems *purely* . . . in terms of diction, structure and point of view, remaining safely inside the realm of the formal" (*CE,* 1:221). And yet, as Fiedler rightly points out, an author's choices regarding the formal elements of his work imply a judgment about the experience he is rendering. Because such judgments have moral ramifications, an amoral criticism is one that is aesthetically irresponsible.

At the time that he was writing this essay, Fiedler tended to see morality and aesthetics as being fundamentally related. "In the realm of fiction," he writes, "to be inept, whether unwittingly or on purpose, is the single unforgivable sin. To be inept is to lie; and for this, time and the critics grant no pardon" (*CE*, 1:222). Fiedler's principal targets here are middlebrow authors such as Leon Uris and Allen Drury and conscious antistylists such as James Jones and Jack Kerouac. Because such writers pander to the smug mediocrity of their audience, they win the sort of popularity and esteem that is denied to more serious and subversive writers. These latter artists usually experience one of two fates: they are either condemned as "dirty writers" or are misread and thus made classics for the wrong reasons. (If this analysis seems to minimize mythopeic power and to denigrate popular taste, it should be noted that Fiedler now considers "No! In Thunder" to be "an insufferably arrogant essay" [*WWL*, 37].)

The nonacceptance of serious fiction by the public is not an expression of prudery (American best-sellers have traditionally exploited sex) or even ignorance (the misreading of writers such as Faulkner and Pasternak is largely a willful act). It is rather a reaction against the perceived morbidity of our best writers. To Fiedler's mind, the morally committed writer is not only a superior craftsman but also an inveterate nay-sayer or iconoclast. Indeed, he argues that "insofar as a work of art is, as art, successful, it performs a negative critical function; for the irony of art in the human situation lies in this: that man—or better, some men—are capable of achieving in works of art a coherence, a unity, a balance, a satisfaction of conflicting impulses which they cannot (but which they desperately long to) achieve in love, family relations, politics." The irony is enhanced by the fact that perfectly realized works of art inevitably represent imperfectly realized aspects of life (love, family, politics, etc.). "The image of man in art, however magnificently portrayed—indeed, precisely when it is most magnificently portrayed—is the image of a failure. There is no way out" (*CE*, 1:225).[1]

Fiedler is most emphatically not referring to what is commonly known as protest literature. Even when such literature is politically courageous, it tends to be a partisan indictment of specific social ills or suspect ideologies. "Even the attack on slavery in Twain's post–Civil War *Huckleberry Finn*—or, for that matter, in Mrs. Stowe's pre–Civil War *Uncle Tom's Cabin*—like an anti-McCarthyite fiction in the recent past or an excoriation of segregation right now, carry with them a certain air of presumptive self-satisfaction, an assurance of being justified by the future" (*CE*, 1:227). Fiedler sees these

works, to the extent that they are regarded simply as protest literature, to be easy or pseudo-no's, really disguised yes's. In contrast,
the real nay-sayer is never partisan. On principle, he is willing to
infuriate his friends as well as his enemies.

What differentiates a truly serious novel such as Saul Bellow's
*The Victim* from such "earnest and humane tracts on anti-Semitism"
as *Focus, Gentleman's Agreement,* and *The Professor's Umbrella* is that
Bellow believes "both Jew and gentile are simultaneously Victim
and Victimizer. . . . Our Jewishness or gentileness, Bellow leaves
us feeling, is *given;* our humanity is what we must achieve" (*CE,*
1:235). It is this striving for the complex, universal, and profoundly
disturbing truth that constitutes the integrity of the serious novelist.
As Melville observed of Hawthorne, such a novelist says "NO! in
thunder." However, "in the end," Fiedler tells us, "the negativist
is no nihilist, for he affirms the void. Having endured a vision of
the meaninglessness of existence, he retreats neither into self-pity
and aggrieved silence nor into a realm of beautiful lies. He chooses,
rather, to render the absurdity which he perceives, to know it and
make it known. To know and to render, however, mean to give
form; and to give form is to provide the possibility of delight—a
delight which does not deny horror but lives at its intolerable heart"
(*CE,* 1:238).

## Song and Story

When Ernest Hemingway declared that all American literature
had begun with *Huckleberry Finn,* he was talking primarily of modern
fiction. The real beginning of the American poetic tradition was
Walt Whitman's *Leaves of Grass.* Whether modern American poets
see themselves as descendants of Whitman or as his mortal enemies
is finally beside the point. He is the touchstone against which our
poetry defines itself, a fact with which even so un-Whitmanic a
figure as Ezra Pound eventually had to come to terms. Indeed,
Whitman's image looms so much larger than life that one suspects
at times that it is larger than art as well; or that Whitman shares
with Poe the dubious distinction of being his own most memorable
creation.

As Fiedler reminds us, to speak of Whitman is to speak of a
many-faceted persona, a sort of cultural Rohrschach test in which
different interest groups see their own compulsions represented. At

various times, Whitman has been seen as the avatar of a new home-grown religion (a sort of "Mary Baker Eddy of American poetry" [*CE,* 1:154]), a prophet of sexual emancipation, and the quintessential democrat. Those who focus on the second of these roles are responding more to an image of swagger and braggadocio than to the tormented homosexual who never made it all the way out of the closet. Even stranger is the appropriation of Whitman by political radicals. That a man who supported capitalism and despised trade unions should become a Marxist saint is surprising. That a poem by such a Yankee Doodle patriot as Whitman should have been placed in the hands of Soviet troops fighting the American Expeditionary Forces in Siberia is nothing short of astounding.

It is certainly a paradox that *Leaves of Grass* was originally conceived of as an anonymous poem. In many ways Whitman would seem to be our least anonymous poet. And yet, to separate the "real" Walt Whitman from the self-created persona of the poetry is no easy task. Perhaps it is necessary only to acknowledge rather than to explicate the disparity between man and myth. If Milton could nearly lose himself in the conventions of the pastoral elegy, Whitman may have achieved a similar self-effacement in the mask of the bard. Not only has Whitman created an ideal speaker, Fiedler argues, but also an ideal audience—"the Beatrice he could never leave off wooing, the Penelope to whom he could never return." Speaking of "Song of Myself," Fiedler writes:

As the hero of [Whitman's] poem is called "I," so the loved one is called "you"; and their vague pronominal romance is the thematic center of "Song of Myself." It is an odd subject for the Great American Poem: the celebration (half-heroic, half-ironic) of the mating between an "I" whose reality is constantly questioned and an even more elusive "you." The latter pronoun in Whitman's verse almost always is followed by the phrase "whoever you are." . . . Unless such a "you" really exists, there is no point, no possibility of converting private "vision" into public "song." It is because Whitman's personal concern on this score coincides with a more general problem that he touches us so deeply. (*CE,* 1:290)

Probably no American poet has celebrated the common man more extravagantly than has Whitman (indeed, that common man may well be the "you" of his poetry). During Whitman's own time, few poets were more contemptuous of popular tastes than was Edgar Allan Poe. And yet, over the years Poe has enjoyed a much wider audience than has Whitman. That this is the case is evidence that what the public most desires in poetry is not populist sentiment but familiar prosody and bathos. Modern poets are automatically condemned to a small readership to the extent that they are guilty of an iconoclastic difficulty. Fiedler is surely right when he says that for some time in the United States "poetry has been . . . not so much bought and read as honored and studied" (*WE*, 179). As a result poets have grown accustomed to a marginal role in society, one that consists of beating a path "back and forth between the classroom and the mad-house" (*WE*, 181).

The irony of the present situation lies in the fact that poetry has ceased to be widely read at a time when people cannot step into an elevator or an office building without being bombarded by Muzak or drive their cars without compulsively turning on the radio. Our biggest celebrities these days are not movie stars but musicians (the most recent version of *A Star Is Born* dealt with the music industry not with Hollywood). What the people who shun poetry but love popular music seem not to realize is that originally all poems were sung and that until recently there was no large-scale distinction between song lyrics and printed verse. But then, the reaction of the populace possesses a certain logic, since poets themselves have for the most part abandoned their role as bards of the people in favor of the more elitist vocation of high priest to an esoteric religion of culture. Has anyone ever actually tried to sing "The Love Song of J. Alfred Prufrock"?

In the nineteenth century, American attitudes toward poetry (and indeed poetry itself) were radically different. In the same year that that chest-thumping egalitarian Walt Whitman published the first edition of *Leaves of Grass,* the conservative and aristocratic Longfellow came out with *The Song of Hiawatha.* It was the latter poem that the people actually took to their hearts. Fiedler tells us that when Longfellow "was invited to the court of Queen Victoria, before bowing to the throne he was obliged to sign autographs for fans in the servants' quarters of the royal household" (*WWL*, 86).

Today Longfellow and other nineteenth-century writers of majority verse (Lowell, Whittier, and Eugene Field are three whom Fiedler mentions by name) have been decanonized.[2] Against elitist protest Whitman has been bootlegged into the curriculum by creative writers who find his influence seminal, and Poe has been reluctantly accepted because of his reputation among the French symbolists. With only the slightest overstatement, however, Fiedler contends that the sole American poet who wrote between the War of 1812 and the Spanish American War to be wholeheartedly endorsed by the critical establishment is Emily Dickinson "since she possessed, among other virtues, that of having been almost entirely unknown in her own time" (*WWL,* 88).

During the period when Fiedler was writing *Waiting for the End* (the early sixties), the divided state of American poetry seemed to be best exemplified by the contrasting figures of Ezra Pound and Robert Frost. Long before he made his celebrated radio broadcasts for Mussolini, Pound had committed a more fundamental treason against American culture. Although Americans have often looked favorably upon the enemies of democracy, Negroes, and Jews, they have been less tolerant of those who violated middle-class notions of artistic decorum. The fact that most Americans who knew Pound to be a traitor and a madman had never read the *Pisan Cantos* or any of the other flagrantly modernist poems written under Pound's influence (e.g., Eliot's *The Waste Land,* Crane's *The Bridge,* and William's *Paterson)* is somehow irrelevant. Because we know in a very general way that modern poetry has come to consist of "fragmented, allusion-laden, imagistic portraits of an atomized world" (*WE,* 185), we implicitly judge Pound when we censure this development.

The poet whom twentieth-century America embraced just as passionately as it repudiated Pound was Robert Frost. Despite his early expatriation in England and his contempt for bourgeois life, Frost was shrewd enough to write in conventional verse forms about subjects that had been regarded as properly poetic since the time of the Romantics. Frost was loved by those "who hated all other living poets . . . [precisely] because he seemed to them a reproach to those others who made them feel inferior with their allusions to Provencal and Chinese poetry, their subverted syntax and fractured logic, their unreasonable war against the iambic, their preference for strange Mediterranean lands and big cities" (*WE,* 188).

Although Fiedler's pop predilections would seem to put him more in the camp of Frost than of Pound, he praises both men for having written "certain lines which no literate American, perhaps no educated man anywhere, will willingly forget" (*WE,* 190). At the same time, he criticizes both for having pursued their own legends so assiduously that they have alienated themselves from certain peo-

ple who will not read them and have just as egregiously endeared
themselves to those who will read (or misread) them for the wrong
reasons.

In our time the novel has certainly fared much better than poetry.
Although its narrative function is now being taken over by movies,
television, journalism, and pulp literature, the mainstream American novel could boast a fairly wide audience until well after World
War II. It began to decline in popularity only after it ceased being
a storytelling medium that reflected the concerns of ordinary people.
Fiedler may well be correct when he argues that the American novel
has traditionally been nonrealistic or even antirealistic, but the dreams
that it embodied were communal property. With the triumph of
modernism and (more recently) of postmodernism, the writing and
reading of fiction has come increasingly to be an elitist exercise.
However, such was not yet the case when Fiedler wrote "Adolescence
and Maturity in the American Novel" in 1955.

In this essay Fiedler sensed that American fiction had come to
the end of an era and was facing an uncertain future. Formerly
revered writers such as Sinclair Lewis, James T. Farrell, and John
Dos Passos seemed passé and others, such as Sherwood Anderson
and John Steinbeck, appeared less formidable than in earlier times.
Although Hemingway and Faulkner were still writing, their recent
work was embarrassingly weak when contrasted with their powerful
earlier novels. Proletarian realism (a genre which, properly speaking,
was neither proletarian nor realistic) had run its course by the end
of the thirties, and its major practitioners—when visible at all—
were seen "in a list of witnesses before a Congressional investigating
committee, or on the masthead of a Luce publication" (CE, 1:198).
Among the more recent novelists to be touted as heirs apparent to
Hemingway and Faulkner were atavistic postnaturalists such as James
Jones and Norman Mailer and sentimental liberals such as John
Hersey and Irwin Shaw. The situation seemed far from encouraging.

At the highbrow level the two most dominant schools of contemporary fiction were associated with *Harper's Bazaar* (here understood as a synecdoche for slick fashion magazines in general) and
*Partisan Review.* To Fiedler's mind, the most important writer of
the former group was Carson McCullers, the most typical Truman
Capote. Fiedler regards the Gothic homosexual sensibility of such
writers as somehow descended from Faulkner's neurotic antifem-
inism. When this sensibility is most camp it "appeals profoundly

to certain rich American women with cultural aspirations, and is therefore sponsored in their salons and published decoratively in magazines that cater to their tastes" (*CE,* 1:201–2).

In contrast, the *Partisan Review* crowd seemed less interested in high style than in moral earnestness. The journal itself had been founded in the thirties by Communists who later broke with the party during Stalin's reign of terror. It flourished (in terms of impact if not circulation) as a forum for independent political thought and for a kind of European (largely Jewish) literary sensibility, which pays homage to James and Faulkner but seems more deeply influenced by Kafka. In Fiedler's opinion the most talented writer to emerge from this group was Saul Bellow. However, despite the specific abilities of Bellow and the general high-mindedness of the editors of *Partisan Review,* the tradition that sustained this journal was more a matter of will than of organic growth. Indeed, "it is hard to see how such a situation can be avoided in a society distinguished by the indifference of the many to the making of its taste, and by an unbridgeable gap between its productive present and its only viable literary past" (*CE,* 1:208).

In early November 1960 Fiedler and his Montana State colleague Seymour Betsky made a pilgrimage to Ketchum, Idaho, to see a living embodiment of America's literary past—the dying novelist Ernest Hemingway. Although the ostensible purpose of the trip was to persuade Hemingway to speak at their university, Fiedler and Betsky were actually "seeking the shrine of a God in whom we were not quite sure we believed" (*CE,* 2:345). The occasion was particularly difficult for Fiedler, because in his critical writing he had balanced his praise of Hemingway with honest censure of the novelist's more glaring faults. (At a symposium in Naples ten years earlier, he had told an Italian admirer of Hemingway: "yes—sometimes he puts down the closest thing to silence attainable in words, but often what he considers reticence is only the garrulousness of the inarticulate" [*CE,* 2:345].) And Hemingway was notorious for reading the critics. When receiving his guests, he said, "Fiedler? Leslie Fiedler. Do you still believe that st-st-stuff about Huck Finn?" (*CE,* 2:349).

One affinity that Fiedler felt with Hemingway was that both men were outsiders who had come to live in and identify with the American West (Montana State was the university from which Robert Jordan had departed for the Spanish Civil War in *For Whom the Bell*

*Tolls*). It was only fitting that he had now returned to Sun Valley
to die, "and it was scarcely ironical that his funeral be held in a
tourists' haven, a place where the West sells itself to all comers"
(*CE,* 2:345).

Although Hemingway had never written a book set in the Mountain West, all of the books that he did write were informed by the
same values as the television Western: "The West he exploited is
the West not of geography but of our dearest and most vulnerable
dreams, not a locale but a fantasy, whose meanings do not change
when it is called Spain or Africa or Cuba. As long as the hunting
and fishing is good. And the women can be left behind." This was
the West of Gary Cooper, an actor with whom Hemingway was as
closely identified as Tennessee Williams with Marlon Brando, and
one whose face, "in its inarticulate blankness, [was] a living equivalent of Hemingway's prose style." Along with many others, Fiedler
"was moved by Hemingway's telegram offering Cooper odds of two
to one that he would 'beat him to the barn [i.e., die first]' " (*CE,*
2:346).

What we get in Fiedler's description of Hemingway ("An Almost
Imaginary Interview: Hemingway in Ketchum") is the picture of a
frail man who is old before his time. We find *TV Guide* and *Reader's
Digest* on his coffee table; and when he tries to play the gracious
host, offering his guests "Tavel—a fine little wine from the Pyre-
nees," he simply degenerates into self-parody. It soon becomes evident that if Hemingway had ever been capable of speaking in public,
those days are now gone. It is difficult enough for him even to
write. At the end of that awkward encounter, the Hemingways
drove their guests back to town to pick up Betsky's car. Among
the chores that Hemingway had to do in town that morning was
go to the bank. But since it was Saturday, the bank was closed,
and Hemingway was reduced to rattling the closed glass doors.
" 'Shit,' he said finally to the dark interior and the empty street,"
Fiedler reports, "and we headed for our car fast, fast, hoping to
close the scene on the first authentic Hemingway line of the morning. But we did not move quite fast enough, had to hear over the
slamming of our car door the voice of Mrs. Hemingway calling to
her husband (he had started off in one direction, she in another),
'Don't forget your vitamin tablets, Daddy' " (*CE,* 2:354).

## Chapter Nine
# The End of the Beginning

If American literature seemed dead in the water in the mid-fifties and on the verge of a sea-change in the early sixties, the new order of things had begun to establish itself well before the seventies were here. Aging Beats such as Allen Ginsberg and William S. Burroughs had become folk heroes to a new generation of dopers; Norman Mailer was in the unaccustomed position of being no more bizarre than the majority of his readers; and J. D. Salinger had lapsed into what promised to be permanent silence. Among the camp Southern Gothicists, Carson McCullers was dead, and Truman Capote was busy promoting himself along with a supposedly new genre of literature called the "nonfiction novel." Over at the *Partisan Review,* Saul Bellow and other middle-aged Jewish radicals had already started down the road to neo-conservatism. However, what was probably the symbolic turning point for our national muse came when, within a year of each other, both Ernest Hemingway and William Faulkner had made it to the barn.

## Requiem for a Genre

Any realistic assessment of the situation would have to concede that the passing of Hemingway and Faulkner did not deprive America of two great geniuses. Each man had dissipated his talent to the point that physical death was somehow anticlimactic. As Fiedler writes, "In a sense, each received the Nobel Prize posthumously, though both lived long enough to accept it with thanks" (*WE,* 9). What the actual departure of Hemingway and Faulkner occasioned was an assessment of what these men had meant to us and how we could get along without them. In approaching this topic, Fiedler suggests that the badness of the later Hemingway and Faulkner is ironically a key to what was most essential about these writers.

If they ended their careers by parodying themselves, it was because their styles were never far from something like parody. At their best both men were capable of savage irony—Faulkner in his depiction of the Snopes family, Hemingway in his Sherwood Anderson travesty *The Torrents of Spring* (a novel for which Fiedler has a rather extravagant regard). "We should not, then, be surprised that, having exhausted the worlds they began by caricaturing (and having succeeded in those very worlds at the same time), the two comic geniuses of our century ended by caricaturing themselves" (*WE,* 10).

Fiedler finds it more than a little ironic that Faulkner should have died just before the region that he immortalized in fiction would become the center of national controversy. The reference here is not just to the general struggle for civil rights in the South, but to the specific confrontation in Faulkner's hometown of Oxford, Mississippi, "where, just after his death, Federal troops were deployed to insure the registration of a single, indifferent Negro student in a less-than-mediocre university. It is as if history itself were subscribing to Faulkner's view of the South—his notion of a baffled aspiration to the tragic, nurtured by dreams and memories, falling away always, in fact, into melodrama or farce" (*WE,* 11). Appropriately enough, a town that had considered Faulkner something of a civic embarrassment during most of his life has not hesitated to capitalize on his memory. For many Americans, the South that Faulkner hated passionately enough to understand, and hence redeem in the alchemy of his art, belongs forever to the town drunk of Oxford, Mississippi.

If Faulkner is an example of the success of failure (he was not widely known at the time that he was doing his best writing and all of his books were out of print by the end of World War II), then Hemingway is more nearly a case of the failure of success. He was, in Fiedler's opinion, both liked and disliked for the wrong reasons: "his truest strengths presented themselves all along in the guise of weaknesses, his most disabling weaknesses in the guise of strengths" (*WE,* 12). Fiedler regards Hemingway's macho posturing as meretricious and diversionary, while his real value was as a poet of terror. (In an earlier essay he had expressed his impatience with "those young writers from Rome or Palermo or Milan who write in translated Hemingwayese about hunting and *grappa* and getting laid—but who have no sense of the nighttime religious anguish which makes Hemingway a more Catholic writer than most modern Italians" [*CE,* 2:345].) The true Hemingway is not so much a bull as a steer, and so it is appropriate that the protagonist of what now seems to be his greatest novel, *The Sun Also Rises,* be impotent.

Hemingway's downfall began when the swagger and bravado that had originally been his defense against the abyss became the standard against which he measured his life and his art. By abandoning the "role of the anti-hero, the despised Steer, in whose weakness lay his true strength, Hemingway became first a fiction of his own contriving, then the creature of articles in newspapers and magazines, as unreal as a movie star or a fashion model. And it was the unreal Hemingway who wrote the later books, creating a series of heroes no more real than himself: men who sought rather than fled unreal wars, and who, in the arms of unreal women, achieved unreal delights" (*WE*, 15). Fiedler suspects that Hemingway's defense became his reality, simply because it is too difficult to sustain the mood of Ecclesiastes, the experience of the void. If a dark night of the soul follows the saint's vision of God, how much darker must the night be "when the initial vision is itself of nothingness" (*WE*, 15). When the pose could no longer be sustained (Hemingway's mind and body were both deteriorating at the end), his only alternative was to leave off vicarious dying for the real thing.

Because Hemingway created a language that has influenced almost all subsequent writers of English (and quite a few other modern tongues as well), his impact on literature has been incredibly diffuse. However, he seems not to have founded a specific school of writers. Fiedler argues that such self-proclaimed Hemingway disciples as John O'Hara, Norman Mailer, and Vance Bourjaily "are less like Hemingway than they think—or, perhaps, only assert" (*WE*, 17). Papa's only obvious literary progeny are hard-boiled writers such as Dashiell Hammett, Raymond Chandler, Mickey Spillane, and Richard S. Prather. Faulkner, on the other hand, wrote in a style that is impossible profitably to imitate, and yet seems to be the father of three separate groups of writers—homosexual dandies such as Truman Capote and Tennessee Williams; Southern ladies such as Katherine Anne Porter, Eudora Welty, and Flannery O'Connor; and "a one-man line of development, stemming from the popular and anti-feminine elements in Faulkner (so oddly transmuted in the first two groups), in the novels of Robert Penn Warren" (*WE*, 18).

Regardless of the nature of their influence, the passing of Hemingway and Faulkner changed the literary cosmos in America, "like, perhaps, the removal of the sky, an atmosphere we were no longer aware we breathed, a firmament we had forgotten sheltered us. The

sky we can pretend, at least, is Heaven; the space behind the sky
we cannot help suspecting is a vacuum" (*WE,* 9).

It is not our purpose here to determine whether the novel is dead
as an art form, only to recognize that by the mid-sixties Fiedler
believed it so. (Although the passing of Hemingway and Faulkner
could not kill an otherwise living genre, the death of these grand
old men forced the critical establishment to consider what lay ahead
for narrative literature.) He was convinced, moreover, that the death
of the novel was implicit in its birth. As a machine-made, mass-
produced, mass-distributed commodity, it was the beginning of
popular art. Thus, it was only a matter of time before technology
would develop storytelling media that did not require print. When
we speak of the death of the novel, we are talking about the end
of the Gutenberg era, because the novel was "the last narrative art-
form invented, or capable of being invented, for *literates*" (*WE,*
172).

At the same time that the popular audience was turning away
from the mainstream novel, fiction writers themselves were beginning more and more to cater to an intellectual and cultural elite.
The net result was to leave a huge vacuum where the traditional
novel once had been. (Because the alienating avant-garde impulses
were largely European—Proust, Mann, Joyce, Kafka, and before
them a thoroughly Europeanized James—the novel survived in
America long after it had begun to decay abroad.) By the mid-
sixties there seemed to be three distinct levels of American fiction.
There were antipopular highbrow novelists such as John Barth and
Thomas Pynchon, writing primarily for academics and other writers.
At the other end of the spectrum were John Jakes and other best-
selling authors of potboilers most readily purchased in the checkout
lines at the supermarket. In between were various middlebrow writers who considered themselves serious artists but who were also
determined to woo the mass audience. Mainstream American novelists from Twain and Howells to Hemingway and Faulkner had
managed to bridge the gap between high and low in a way that
more recent middlebrows could only aspire to do.

By the early eighties, all three levels of American fiction were
not only going strong but were busy subdividing. "When the novel
dies, it leaves behind not a vacuum but a proliferating swarm of
competing subgenres, each clamoring for recognition" (*WWL,* 80).
The Association of American Book Publishers acknowledged this

fact in 1979 by announcing that it would no longer give a single award for fiction, but instead would bestow separate prizes for the best "Children's Book," "Science Fiction," "Mystery," "Western," and "First Novel." Although the howls from elitist writers and critics caused the association to cut back on this list, the point had been made. Fiedler notes that the association was trying to keep more traditional and popular fiction from being ignored in favor of experimental postmodernist works; however, no provision was made for considering the supermarket schlock which are surely the most salable of all books. What the publishers had in mind was "the work of 'serious,' undisturbingly respectable authors, who remain as unaware as they that traditional narrative fiction is obsolete" (*WWL,* 81).

## Reading It New

While Fiedler was busy pronouncing the last rites over the novel, he was finding surprising vitality in the long-moribund genre of American poetry. Consequently, *Waiting for the End* concludes with some enthusiastic comments about those whom Fiedler considered to be the most promising American poets of the late fifties and early sixties, along with appropriate homage to their more influential predecessors. (Although it is probable that Fiedler now considers that enthusiasm to have been premature and unvindicated, it seemed plausible enough at the time.) The most valuable part of his discussion, however, is "The Unbroken Tradition," an essay in which he traces four continuous lines of development in American verse. These bear a striking resemblance to the regional genres of the American novel delineated in *The Return of the Vanishing American.*

At first glance, the influence of the most popular American poet of the nineteenth century—Henry Wadsworth Longfellow—would seem to be limited to his own time. No modern American poet of any stature sees himself as an inheritor of the Longfellow tradition. That tradition, however, has blended itself with a whole body of popular poetry and song that is "the nearest thing to a common culture we possess" (*WE,* 197).[1] Such Longfellow chestnuts as "The Children's Hour" and "The Village Blacksmith" are as well known as "The Night Before Christmas" and the songs of Stephen Collins Foster. If highbrow modernists shun the didactic content and conventional prosody of Longfellow, it is with an awareness that they are defining themselves *against* the model that he provides. As Fiedler notes, whenever such modernists "turn from nostalgic and evocative parody to brutal satire and burlesque, mocking popular culture at the point where it becomes best-selling poetry, they are likely to be thinking of Henry Wadsworth Longfellow" (*WE*, 197).

What Longfellow represented to the mass audience of his day was a genteel version of "culture." He had studied at the best universities in Europe and was professionally engaged in elevating the tastes of the sons of America's ruling class as the first professor of modern literature at Harvard. Because he was a best-selling poet, ordinary men and women could also get in on the act. That the populace took to him much more than to the egalitarian Whitman suggests that Americans are motivated less by class solidarity than by a desire for upward mobility. Along with the accessibility of his verse, Longfellow's cultural elitism assured his popularity. As the purveyor of what was taken to be a European standard of culture, he was our quintessential Eastern poet.

Because he was both a Gothicist and a dandy, Edgar Allan Poe can be seen as the father of a significant tradition in Southern literature. Like Longfellow, Poe was a highbrow who would experience the ironic fate of being scorned by a later generation of elitist critics while being loved by a mass audience. Also like Longfellow, he wrote highly musical verse and sought to domesticate certain aspects of European culture. What differentiates him from his even more popular contemporary, and ultimately makes him more a Southern than an Eastern poet, are the content and purpose of his verse. Poe's Europe was an exotic and sensational dream landscape which existed more in nightmare than in geography, and seemed fundamentally alien to the middlebrow religion of high culture exemplified by Longfellow. Also, the music of Poe's verse was not simply an ornament for aphoristic or platitudinous thought (as was too often the case with Longfellow's poetry), but rather a synesthetic device for creating moods for which there was no prose equivalent.

Although Poe's influence on highbrow American poetry is considerably more extensive than that of Longfellow, he made it into the canon in a rather roundabout way. He has always been a favorite poet of children and young adolescents, but adult Americans have found him "at once too banal and too unique, too decadent and too revolutionary, too vulgar and too subtle, all of which is to say, too American, for us to bear except as reflected in the observing eye of

Europe" (*WE*, 199). And it is through that eye that he has come back to us. Sophisticated modern poets such as Pound and Eliot, who would regard Poe as a crude versifier, freely acknowledge the influence of Poe's French admirers Baudelaire and Mallarmé. What all of these poets share is an antirationalist symbolic imagination that sometimes verges into surrealism.[2]

As we have already seen, our most self-consciously *American* poet was Walt Whitman. For Whitman, being an American meant severing one's cultural ties with Europe and finding poetic inspiration in the indigenous materials of our own country (he considered the United States themselves to be the greatest poem). If Longfellow regarded the poet as a moral teacher and Poe saw him as a total aesthete, Whitman was more inclined to view the poetic vocation as a priestly calling. His religion was not the bourgeois Protestantism of Longfellow or the compulsive diabolism of Poe, but a kind of inverted mysticism that found transcendence through a joyous immersion in sensual experience. As perhaps the most enthusiastic of our nineteenth-century American Adams, he was a totally original poet who eschewed such trappings of the past as conventional prosody. He invented for America the free-verse poem that was written in long lines scarcely distinguishable from impassioned prose.

Although Whitman lived his entire life in the East, he was mythologically a poet of the American West. Because the West is always coextensive with whatever might be the current frontier, it maintains a fixed archetypal significance even as its physical boundaries change. As a poetic personality, Whitman projected himself forward in both time and space. It was only through conquering time and space that one could achieve cosmic unity at a higher level of being. To find the passage not only to India, but to more than India, was ultimately the manifest destiny of the spirit. Whitman's truest descendants were not only those who emulated his style in life and art, but those who shared his passion for exploration—actual Westerners such as Carl Sandburg and Vachel Lindsay and spiritual pioneers such as Allen Ginsberg and his fellow Beats.

The final line of American verse that Fiedler identifies is the least obvious but most enduring and continuous of the four. Although it actually begins with Edward Taylor, Fiedler identifies it with Emerson, because "it is Emerson who brought it to full consciousness, at the very moment when the schools of Longfellow and Poe and Whitman were defining themselves for the first time" (*WE*, 210–11). This line runs from Emerson through Emily Dickinson, to Edwin Arlington Robinson, Robert Frost, and the early Robert Lowell. (Because Taylor's verse was not discovered until the 1930s, it apparently represents a confluence rather than an influence.) Although Longfellow and Emerson were both New England Brahmins, Longfellow was identified more with cosmopolitan Boston and Emerson with provincial Concord. In other words, Emerson and company are not Eastern but Northern poets (did not Robert Frost publish a volume called *North of Boston?*).

"For Emerson," Fiedler writes, "the poet is neither dandy nor agitator nor domesticated paraclete; he is, rather, a lonely philosopher or magician; a rebel, perhaps, as much as Whitman's mythical poet, but one, in Frost's phrase, 'too lofty and original to rage' " (*WE*, 212). This line of poetry, particularly in the hands of Robinson and Frost, always scanned and frequently told a story. Moreover, it is about the only body of American verse that deals with nature as observed reality rather than as symbolic construct (to some extent this can be said of the poetry of the agrarian South as well). If the poetry of Whitman is based on a European myth of America and that of Longfellow and Poe on an American myth of Europe, the Emersonian line is more authentically homegrown. Because it lacks the *chutzpah* of Whitman, the *pudeur* of Poe, and the transparency of Longfellow, it is a tradition that critics have found difficult to pigeonhole. Although Fiedler's comments are themselves inconclusive, they do what all criticism should do for the familiar—allow us to read it new.

## Chapter Ten
# Beyond Literacy

The youth culture of the sixties effected profound changes in the university. With the post–World War II baby boom coming of age and draft deferments putting a premium on college attendance, enrollments swelled. This in turn created a need for more faculty, which was satisfied by an influx of persons who in any other era might not have found or even sought employment in the academy. These demographic factors, combined with nationwide social unrest, led to a radical reevaluation of the very premises of university education, particularly in the liberal arts. Even conventional elitist professors were experiencing a crisis of confidence. Not only did they let their hair grow, forsake academic tweed for blue jeans or bell bottoms, and begin to smoke pot and sleep with their students, but they took the decidedly more revolutionary step of opening up the canon of their disciplines to the pop culture of the young. It would be tempting to see Leslie Fiedler as simply a part of this trend; however, he was a barbarian long before his colleagues began to "green" and has remained an outlaw long after it has ceased to be fashionable to be one. As Fiedler himself has pointed out, the only alternative to biting the hand that feeds one is "biting the ass one kisses" (*CE,* 1:xiv).

## The Dirtiest Beast of the Age

In his 1955 essay "The Middle Against Both Ends," Fiedler proudly declared: "I am surely one of the few people pretending to intellectual respectability who can boast that he has read more comic books than attacks on comic books" (*CE,* 2:415). Although the controversy to which he is addressing himself here is by now dated (comic books having gone the way of Cinerama and hardtop convertibles), the phenomenon of censorship is still very much with us. While highbrow intellectuals will go to the barricades to defend *Ulysses* or *Lady Chatterley's Lover* from the philistine attacks of the Parent Teachers Association and other middlebrow defenders of civic virtue, those same critics often join in the assault upon popular culture. Although the highbrows may have certain First Amendment reservations about outright suppression, their defense of standards effectively anathematizes literature that has failed to make it into the canon. What the middlebrow rejects on ethical grounds, the highbrow repudiates for aesthetic reasons.

Fiedler suspects that the middlebrow ultimately desires a homogenous culture that has no room for either high or pop art. In part, this desire is bred out of a democratic faith that finds different levels of art suspiciously redolent of a class system. (Although Fiedler is also a democrat, he finds freedom and diversity preferable to the uniformity of a melting-pot culture.) This democratic faith, however, conceals the anxiety that one's own cultural attainments are tenuous. The high art of the avant-garde represents a level of sophistication to which the middlebrow has yet to rise. Conversely, the pop culture of the lower classes suggests "to him a condition to which he might easily relapse." Thus, the logic of the middlebrow runs something like this: "Since he cannot on his own terms explain to himself why anyone should choose any level but the highest (that is, his own), the failure of the vulgar seems to him the product of mere ignorance and laziness—a crime! And the rejection by the advanced artist of his canons strikes him as a finicking excess, a pointless and unforgivable snobbism. . . . The fear of the vulgar is the obverse of the fear of excellence, and both are aspects of the fear of difference: symptoms of a drive for conformity on the level of the timid, sentimental, mindless-bodiless genteel" (CE, 2:428).

In What Was Literature? Fiedler traces the impulse to censorship all the way back to Plato's contention that "art is incitement rather than therapy" (WWL, 42). Although good liberals tend to scoff at this notion when it is used to suppress erotic literature, they have no compunction about deploring violence in the media (comics were particularly vulnerable because they combined sex and violence). This has led to such absurdities as the bowdlerization of Mother Goose and the Brothers Grimm, as well as to attacks on Fiedler's favorite cop shows, Baretta, Kojak, and Starsky and Hutch. It wasn't very long before various stigmatized interest groups (blacks, women, Poles, Hispanics, homosexuals, and the handicapped) began to assert their sensitivities. This has not only resulted in the suppression of Amos 'n Andy and Little Black Sambo (regrettable enough in and of itself), but to protests against everything from Shakespeare's The

*Merchant of Venice* to Griffith's *The Birth of a Nation* and Twain's *Adventures of Huckleberry Finn.* To all book-burners with political axes to grind, Fiedler cries: enough already!

His real targets, however, are those with cultural axes to grind. Fiedler's intriguing theory is that the elite canon of literature is the special preserve not so much of the old WASP guardians of culture as of the nouveau academics—*arriviste* Jews and Eastern European ethnics whose entire claim to cultural respectability lies in their defense of high literature. Such individuals are typically not "scholars" in the traditional sense of the term. They are "critics" who began their careers by defending avant-garde literature in "little magazines" and cultist reviews, rather than writing about the classics in academic journals. Once they secured a place in the academy, however, they used it to enforce their own orthodoxy. It is simply another case of battered children growing up to be child beaters.

In most universities the study of literature either is or aspires to be an esoteric craft practiced by a cultural elite. One's advancement in academic stature is measured by the extent to which he (or occasionally she) is removed from the task of dealing with ordinary students. As a graduate student, one is forced to teach freshman composition (not because it is the easiest course to teach, but because persons of higher academic rank consider it a burden to be shunned at all costs). Promotion usually carries with it reduced teaching loads and courses consisting increasingly of upper-division and graduate students who have been indoctrinated with the tastes and jargon of whatever happens to be the prevailing critical orthodoxy. In other words, we have a kind of self-perpetuating guild system that is financially supported by the mass of people (taxpayers if it is a public university, alumni if it is a private institution) who are outside the guild but who pay it the sort of homage also rendered to opera and ballet (as a Texas oilman said of one such venture: "I'll give you $100,000 just so long as I don't have to go to the son of a bitch").

Those (such as Fiedler) who challenge the elitism of traditional literary study are accused of subverting the standards of high culture, of wanting to "open the gates to the barbarians." To this charge Fiedler simply replies: "I *am* a barbarian, already within the gates" (*WWL,* 112). Once the academy allowed courses in living languages (rather than confining literature to a study of the classics), the crucial concession had been made. As more and more recent texts were admitted to the canon, or at least deemed worthy of study, "criticism" replaced "scholarship" as the means for determining literary excellence. Fiedler goes a step farther by suggesting that there may be a more adequate standard of criticism than one that would censure technically inept but mythically powerful works of art. For having the temerity to say this, he has been branded by Hugh Kenner as "the man who wants [literature] dead."[1]

The point, of course, is that literature (at least as we have known it) is already dead. It began to die when it was taken out of the court and salon and made available to ordinary people in the eighteenth century. The attempt of Henry James and his followers to redeem the novel for high art, like the attempt of cineasts to make film into an esoteric medium, did not undo the cultural democratizing and leveling initiated by Samuel Richardson and company. The populace still had its mass-produced body of song and story (the very fact of mass production differentiates popular culture from folk art); the elite had simply laid claim to more rarefied texts within the same genres enjoyed by their less sophisticated brethren. Moreover, these texts had ceased to be final forms in and of themselves. The poetry and fiction of the elite is written not to be read for its own sake, but to be studied in the academy (frequently in courses in "creative writing"). Similarly, the poetry of the people becomes song lyrics and their fiction television shows and movies.

It might be objected that Fiedler is fighting a battle that has already been partially won. Many universities have courses in American studies and popular culture, and much academic writing is done in these disciplines. However, this represents, at best, a foot in the door. When pop courses are offered, it is frequently a cynical attempt to boost enrollments rather than an admission of the academic legitimacy of such courses. Professors who teach and publish in this area (when they are not certified pedants who are merely slumming) are generally regarded as dilettantes who couldn't make it in the world of "real scholarship."

As long as popular literature remains segregated from the rest of the curriculum, it will continue to be stigmatized as less worthy than the more canonical texts. It is only when popular culture is integrated with high literature in courses that are organized historically or thematically that we can create an "English for everyone: an introduction to works of the imagination over which all humankind can weep, laugh, shudder, and be titillated; communal dreams, shared hallucinations, which in a time when everything else tends to divide us from each other join us together, men and women, adults and children, educated and uneducated, black and white, yellow and brown—even, perhaps, teachers and students" (*WWL,* 114).

## Remaking the Canon

Fiedler argues strenuously (perhaps protesting too much) that he is not forsaking the evaluative role of the critic. The fact that some works of art are superior to others is something that he has never doubted. Even the least sophisticated consumers of art express their opinions and preferences, a task for which no arcane critical vocabulary is needed. The responsible critic, however, must offer more than exclamations of approval or distaste (e.g., "wow" or "ugh"). He must be able to tell us why *Jonathan Livingston Seagull* is "pretentious, banal, and essentially stupid," while *Huckleberry Finn* is "subtle and mythically resonant, yet capable of moving a child of ten" (*WWL,* 126). However, to do so requires an appeal to some standard beyond aesthetics and ethics as those terms are commonly understood.

The hazard inherent in traditional aesthetics is that it leads us to the artificial distinction between high and low art against which Fiedler has been railing. The problem with ethical criticism is that it leads toward censorship. As Fiedler has amply demonstrated, the temptation to use literature on behalf of noble ideals and to suppress those works that preach an alien gospel is not limited to the "know nothing" fringes of the radical right but also afflicts "enlightened liberals." The Aristotelian notion of catharsis is certainly a clever means of dealing with those Platonists who would impose censorship upon us for our own good, and the Arnoldian contention that literature instructs as well as delights may even persuade some moralists that the poet is a civic asset. In our heart of hearts, however, we know that the glory of literature lies in the fact that it is every bit as dangerous and subversive as its worst enemies claim.

If ethics and aesthetics are somehow inadequate measures of the value of art, perhaps simple popularity would do the trick. Certainly, in a society where the majority is entrusted with crucial political and marketing decisions, there is something to be said for leaving artistic decisions up to a plebiscite. Great literature would, by definition, consist of the novels that stayed longest on the best-

sellers list, the songs that were played most often, and the movies
with the highest box office gross. Such a position, however, does
not close the gap between majority and minority art; but, by opting
"for the former rather than the latter, . . . [it simply stands]
elitism on its head" (*WWL*, 116). (Persons making a claim for such
radical populism frequently cite Tolstoy's celebration of folk culture
in his essay *What Is Art?*) Fiedler ultimately rejects this stance, just
as he does the elitist position, "not only because each in its own
way restricts the full freedom of literature, but because each unconsciously *lies* about the works it seeks to defend" (*WWL*, 129).

The way out of this impasse is for all critics to become myth
critics, that is, to focus on those subconscious and unarticulated
sources of appeal that cause certain works of art to move large
numbers of people (how this differs from popularity more crassly
conceived, Fiedler does not say). Because these sources of appeal
exist irrespective of the formal excellence of the works in which they
are embodied, critics will find themselves "speaking less of theme
and purport, structure and texture, signified and signifier, metaphor
and metonymy, and more of myth, fable, archetype, fantasy, magic
and wonder" (*WWL*, 140). What is most important is that the
critic not murder to dissect, but maintain and communicate his
own sense of excitement in the presence of literature. Longinus
referred to this quality as the sublime (or so he has usually been
translated). Fiedler prefers the term *ekstasis*, "meaning ecstasy or
rapture or transport, a profound alteration of consciousness in which
the normal limits of flesh and spirit seem to dissolve" (*WWL*, 139).

Phenomenologically, it is perhaps easiest to see how *ekstasis* works
if we consider four genres of pop literature where the attempt to
evoke a particular audience reaction is most blatant: (1) sentimental
tearjerkers; (2) horror stories; (3) hard-core erotica; and (4) low comedy. "There is a real sense in which all four of these can be regarded
as 'pornography,' since they titillate by infringing deeply revered
taboos and impel us toward some kind of orgasmic release, ranging
from tears to a scream, from uncontrollable laughter to actual eja-
culation" (*WWL*, 134). Presumably, the same qualities that excite
such responses in the customers of "pornography" operate at a more
subtle level in what we have chosen to call high art.

Although Fiedler has dealt with all of these genres at various
times, his comments on them in *What Was Literature?* tend to be
cursory. One can infer, however, that he regards low comedy and

horror stories as having the most universal appeal of all the branches of pop literature. (Sentimental or "handkerchiefly" porn, from Samuel Richardson to today's soaps, excites the particular enthusiasm of women, whereas hard-core erotica is largely a male preserve.) This is because children most readily respond to fun and fright; and since we all started out as kids, what appeals to them should appeal to something in us, regardless of how buried it might be. Indeed, Fiedler seems to think that one of the functions of art is to allow us to regress to an infantile level, and one of its chief rewards, *"unearned instant gratification"* (*WWL,* 138).

As Fiedler notes in his 1969 essay "Cross the Border, Close the Gap," one of the consequences of the breakup of modernism has been the parodic rediscovery of pop forms in high literature. Erotic pornography, for example, surfaced everywhere when standards were relaxed in the sixties. Not only were such earlier classics as *Lady Chatterley's Lover* and *Tropic of Cancer* admitted into the country, but we began homegrowing products as various as Vladimir Nabokov's *Lolita,* Terry Southern's *Candy,* and William S. Burroughs's *Naked Lunch.* Appropriately, the most controversial and sensational bestseller of the late sixties was Philip Roth's hilariously pornographic *Portnoy's Complaint.*

If the highbrow pornography of the sixties can be seen as a joining of erotica and low comedy, horror and sentimentality have continued to thrive almost exclusively in the realm of pop literature (Stephen King and his various imitators having made millions from the former and the various pseudonymous "romance" novelists hundreds of millions from the latter). The other forms of pop that seemed to be crossing the border into high lit by the end of the sixties were the Western (which Fiedler had treated in *The Return of the Vanishing American*) and that mutation of the Western, science fiction.

Although sci-fi had always been considered a legitimate genre for highbrow British writers (such as H. G. Wells, Aldous Huxley, George Orwell, C. S. Lewis, William Golding, and Anthony Burgess), it had long been relegated to a cultural ghetto in America. In the sixties, however, this long-despised medium attracted the talents of such prominent American novelists as William S. Burroughs and John Barth, while the previously hardcore science-fictionist Kurt Vonnegut, Jr., passed into the canon of critically accepted mainstream novelists. (As with erotica and the Western, science fiction was redeemed for high literature by being made the object of parody.) As Fiedler notes in the introduction to *In Dreams Awake,* his own anthology of science fiction: "a basic appeal of the genre surely lies in its creation of technologically oriented mythologies to replace the older ones made obsolete by science. In order to survive, however, such mythologies had to be presented as if they were rooted not in 'wonder' and dreams but in 'extrapolation' from scientific 'fact.' Science fiction may be a literature of dreams, but its dreams are those of men dreaming they are awake" (*I,* 15).

Fiedler began his career by challenging the critical consensus. However, since the breakup of the formalist hegemony in the sixties, there has been no consensus, only a multitude of critical stances (including Fiedler's) seeking to fill the vacuum. For those of us who make our living teaching the literary canon but also enjoy popular culture the prospect of crossing the border and closing the gap is undeniably appealing. The most satisfying courses I have offered have been interdisciplinary classes in American culture that have employed novels, nonfiction narratives, and films without an obsessive regard for elitist standards. Therefore, I approve of the direction in which Fiedler is heading. And yet, the rationale and methodology he uses in getting there raise some difficulties.

To begin with, the notion of "ecstatics" smacks of the subjectivism touted by Walter Pater and company back during the British fin de siècle period. Even though Fiedler leavens his subjectivism with a democratic faith lacking in his British counterparts, I am not sure that he has identified a new set of objective standards to replace the old one that he has rejected. I believe Rod McKuen's poetry inferior to Dante's and Erich Segal's fiction less entertaining than Leslie Fiedler's, but the concept of ecstatics gives me no vocabulary with which to persuade others that they should share my preferences. When Fiedler pushes beyond ecstatics to the source of literary ecstasy, which he identifies as myth, he suggests a way out of the impasse, but at the expense of limiting the range of his criticism.

Old-line scholars have traditionally asserted that great literature is that which has survived the test of time. What the formalists attempted to do was to articulate critical standards to explain *why* great literature has survived and to identify those contemporary works that have what it takes to make it into the canon. In practice, however, formalism is less than totally successful. Some works survive which presumably should have died, while others that should have thrived have faded from memory. By suggesting that works of literature either fade or endure because of qualities more deeply interfused than the technical excellence of the language in which they are written, myth critics such as Fiedler are probably closer to the truth than are formalists who reject certain undeniably great writers (as the neoclassical critics did with Shakespeare and as Yvor Winters has done with practically everyone) because they do not measure up to certain prescriptive standards, or else accept them (as Cleanth Brooks does in *The Well Wrought Urn*) because they can be sufficiently misread to satisfy those same standards.

The advantage that formalism seems to give its adherents over both the old-line scholar and the myth critic is the ability to judge contemporary works by the same ontological criteria applied to the classics. The scholar simply says that we cannot know ahead of time what will survive, while the myth critic makes his predictions by examining current works for the presence of ancient archetypes. However, it should be obvious that some renderings of myth and fable are more successful than others. Why, for example, has Shakespeare outlasted other playwrights who have dealt with similar themes?

I suspect that Hugh Kenner is close to the answer when he asserts that "the greatest literary works—the *Iliad, Hamlet,*—owe their distinction to . . . the union of a powerful myth with expression just as powerfully adequate."[2] Some works have survived in the academy simply because they were well written; others have survived in popular esteem simply because they were mythically potent. Formalists can help us appreciate the former, and myth critics the latter. No doubt, we should study both. But what we should never lose sight of is the fact that the best literature is that which unites us at the highest rather than the lowest common denominator.

## Chapter Eleven

# The Critic Abroad

Although Fiedler's primary critical endeavors have been in the area of American literature, he is familiar with the work of classic British and continental writers (his doctoral dissertation, for example, was on John Donne). This familiarity creates a rich context for his discussion of our native literary tradition, a fact to which any reader of *Love and Death in the American Novel* can readily attest. A more comprehensive study of Fiedler's criticism would certainly examine his essays on I. L. Peretz, Franz Kafka, Cesare Pevase, and Robert Louis Stevenson (all in *No! In Thunder*) and his recent book on the British science fiction writer Olaf Stapledon. For our purposes, however, it will be sufficient to focus on what he has said about the two major writers of the Western world—Dante Alighieri and William Shakespeare.

## Stoned on Your Love

Despite his best efforts to appear outrageously nonacademic, Fiedler will occasionally do something that proves his ability to compete on the scholarly turf claimed by his highbrow detractors. Perhaps his most virtuoso performance in this regard is his translation and discussion of Dante's sestina to the Lady Pietra. In an age when poetic translation is once again being regarded as an art form in its own right, Fiedler demonstrates (at least with this one poem) a sensitivity to nuance that exceeds that of the sestina's other major translator, Dante Gabriel Rossetti.

Because of its rigid pattern of repetitions, the sestina as a genre is more dependent than most other poetic forms on the tongue in which in is written. With Dante's sestina, for example, it is necessary to know that "Pietra" is both the proper name of the lady being addressed and an allusion to *petra,* the Italian word for stone. What Dante is suggesting, then, is the rigidity of the woman who rejects his love. At a purely denotative level *Donna Pietra* equals Mistress Stone; however, connotatively *donna* is used to imply a more exalted station than can be conveyed by "mistress" or even (for modern readers, anyway) "lady," the latter of which was Rossetti's choice. Fiedler settles upon the word "queen," because its evocation of high rank is unambiguous and because it allows for a series of monorhymes that produce the English equivalent of the prosodic effect created by Dante's Italian. What is lost in both Rossetti's and Fiedler's translations is the pun on "Pietra," since the English surname of "Stone" apparently struck both translators as too contrived.

The first stanza asserts the constancy of the lover, and the second stanza the rigidity of his beloved (which bespeaks an equal but opposite steadfastness). The link between these two concepts is the adverb *similemente,* which had been routinely ignored by previous translators. In effect, Dante is saying "quite as he remains the sole note of spring in winter, she remains the last vestige of winter in the spring. It is no more possible to make her love than to make him cease from loving" (*CE,* 1:253). Then, in the first line of the second stanza, Fiedler obliquely comments on the disparity between the lady's youth and her status for the poet by translating *nova donna* as "little queen." The irony implied in this juxtaposition is all but lost in Rossetti's more pedestrian "youthful lady."

The third stanza opens with four conventionally sweet lines that depict the beloved as a lady with leafy garland and golden curls. As Fiedler notes, in his translation of these lines he has "tried to out-Rossetti Rossetti . . . with a diction quite mannered and verging on the cliché" (*CE,* 1:254). (One rather nice touch is his repetition of "love" as both noun and verb in line four: "Love loves to lounge there in its shade.") This is done to make the shock of the last two lines, in which the beloved is transformed into the warden of the lover's passion, all the more striking. Moreover, in terms of both sound and sense, Fiedler's final line, "More stubborn even than calcareous stone," is more satisfying than Rossetti's "Faster than between walls of granite-stone."

Stanza 4 begins with what seem to be two commonplace lines of praise to the beloved. The Italian, however, hints at a paradox that is anything but commonplace: "[T]he fact that a single word means both 'jewel' and 'rock' [implies] that the magic of the lady, her essential power, is inseparable from the very stoniness which baffles her lover" (*CE,* 1:254–55). Rossetti's "She is more bright than is a precious stone" ignores the paradox. Better, but still unsatisfactory, is Fiedler's rendering: "Her beauty's magic mocks the precious

stone." The rest of the stanza has the whimpering poet flee from
the severity of the lady; as Fiedler would have it: "To find my
freedom from this kind of queen."

Stanza 5 presents what Fiedler interprets to be the lover's wishful
vision of the lady but what Rossetti translates (or mistranslates) as
actual fact. Fiedler provides additional support for his version by
pointing out that the adversative conjunction that begins stanza 6
makes sense only if the depiction of the beloved in stanza five is
read as fantasy rather than memory. "In my fantasy, Dante is saying,
I have imagined the *Donna Pietra* in love, but in fact I know her
to be incapable of being kindled" (*CE,* 1:256).

The perception of the lady changes once again as stanza 6 depicts
her as "this sprig, too moist and green." The term "sprig" suggests
a sense of youthfulness absent from the more general "wood," while
the adjectives "moist" and "green" imply that that youthfulness has
not yet been inflamed by sexual ardor. "Stone or sprig, she is not
a *'bella donna,'* 'a fair and proper queen,' but an unawakened child,
still ignorant of that ultimate obligation of her sex" (*CE,* 1:256).
Stanza 6 closes with the focus returning again to the lover. In order
to see where the skirts of his beloved cast their shade, he is willing
to sleep on stone. In Italian this hyperbole is redeemed from cliché
by the fact that his beloved is named Pietra (stone). Beyond even
the sexual implication, however, is the reality that in death one
does indeed sleep in stone.

The delicate balance of hope and despair is maintained in the
*congedo* (or three-line resolution) of the poem. Here, the lover imagines the "lovely green" of his "little queen" annulling the "blackest
shade" of the hills "as a stone is drowned in grass." The most
optimistic interpretation of these lines would hold that "it is by
virtue of [the lady's] greenness that she has a power over the power
of blackness, overwhelming it as hope triumphs over death and as
the living grass covers insentient stone" (*CE,* 1:258). And yet, we
must also remember that grass is the symbol of mortality, as well
as the emblem of springtime, and that the lady herself is Pietra.
Consequently, "the notion of a new life covering lifeless rock threatens to blur into the image of a dead girl committed to earth" (*CE,*
1:259). It is with that tragic, unresolvable ambivalence that the
lover's true dilemma is finally revealed.

## The Shakespearean Other

If his work on Dante exposes an unsuspected scholarly side of Fiedler's muse, *The Stranger in Shakespeare* is what his attackers would regard as an all too typical example of special pleading. It is not necessary to share this view to realize that, when Fiedler chose to apply his pet theories about American literature to the most highly admired and widely discussed writer in the English language, he was looking for trouble.[1] And yet, because Shakespeare is such a familiar figure, inspired misreadings of his plays and sonnets are frequently more illuminating than are safe and conventional analyses. In his particular study, Fiedler examines four different types of outsiders in the Shakespearean canon—the woman, the Jew, the Moor, and the New World savage.

Before turning to the plays, however, Fiedler makes some inferences about Shakespeare's view of love by examining the songs and sonnets contained in his first published volume *The Passionate Pilgrim*. This book, printed by William Jaggard in 1599, includes what are now known as sonnets 138 and 144, three poems from *Love's Labor's Lost*, four sonnets on the theme of Venus and Adonis, and eleven other pieces of verse. Although the authenticity of some of the contents is subject to debate, the appearance of Shakespeare's name on the title page suggests to Fiedler's satisfaction that the entire book reflects Shakespeare's general point of view. Particularly revealing is sonnet 144. "Beginning as an account of one who would divide his love in two, directing all that is noble in it toward one object, all that is vile toward another, it ends with his discovery of the two in each other's arms—the noble contaminated by the vile" (*SIS,* 19).

What makes this poem more than just a discourse on the ambiguity of passion is the fact that Shakespeare makes the object of his angelic love a fair youth and of his diabolic passion a dark lady. He thus resolves one age-old dilemma: "that between the popular-orthodox conception of woman as temptress and the courtly view of her as savior. By loving a boy rather than a daughter of Eve, Shakespeare insists, one can find salvation." Or rather the illusion of salvation. When the poet finds his two loves in each other's arms, he realizes the hopelessness of his idealized passion: "since there is no pure masculine principle, no male is immune to the evil impulse represented by the female" (*SIS*, 37).

The stranger, according to Fiedler's definition, is one who resembles us closely enough to be recognizable as a member of the human family but who seems alien in other important respects. For men, the original stranger is the woman. The attempt to come to terms with her presence in "a culture whose notion of the human is defined by males" (*SIS*, 45) takes many different forms, the simplest and most vulgar of which is female impersonation. This phenomenon, which survives today principally in tawdry burlesque routines, is both consistent with one of the central historical impulses behind all drama (the desire to express one's fascination with the stranger) and a remnant of one of the customs of Shakespeare's time (that of boys' playing girls' parts). The various levels of sexual identity in Elizabethan comedy become even more confused when female characters assume the disguise of men. In *As You Like It*, for example, "the boy who has been playing Rosalind playing she is Ganymede playing Rosalind, steps out of his role and stage-sex to speak the Epilogue. And though in his-her wedding dress still, he-she informs the audience that 'If I were a woman I would kiss as many of you as had beards that pleased me, complexions that liked me, and breaths that I defied not' " (*SIS*, 47).

However, long before he developed the sophisticated technique displayed in *As You Like It*, Shakespeare was obsessed with the woman as alien. In his first play—*Henry VI, part 1*—he introduces three diabolic Frenchwomen (the Countess of Auvergne, Margaret of Anjou, and Joan of Arc) who are all "bent on betraying the male champion of the English" (*SIS*, 47), and all of whom could have been portrayed by the same actor. Of these, the most significant mythically is Joan. Since she has been canonized by the Roman church and can claim such distinguished literary admirers as Freidrich Schiller, Bernard Shaw, Jean Anouilh, Eugene Sue, and Mark Twain, it is at the very least a novelty to observe Shakespeare's depiction of Joan as a demonic transvestite who was indeed guilty of the charge of witchcraft. Of course, this characterization tells us less about the historical Joan than about Shakespeare's view of women. At a time when renewed interest in the occult makes it again possible to believe in witchcraft, this long-neglected play of Shakespeare's apprenticeship is winning a new and appreciative audience.

In *The Merchant of Venice* we also see women dressing as men, but without the homoerotic overtones of *As You Like It* or the demonic ones of *Henry VI,* part 1. The stranger in this dark comedy or problem play is not the woman, but the Jew. In his discussion of *The Merchant of Venice* Fiedler tries to rescue the mythic character of Shylock from those who would simply make him into a victim of anti-Semitism or would condemn Shakespeare for not having done so. In the story of Shylock and his daughter Jessica, Fiedler argues, Shakespeare has grafted "onto a pre-Christian folk tale elements derived from the official mythology of the Christian Church, though much altered in the course of popular transmission" (*SIS,* 117).

Specifically, Shylock is a variation on Abraham, the Jewish father with a knife in his hand. (Because the Jews have been blamed for killing Christ, Abraham is always remembered by Christians at the point of sacrificing his son, rather than at the moment of reprieve.) In contrast, Jessica is the Jewish maiden who is a good, even redemptive, person to the extent that she is a bad (i.e., treacherous) daughter to her Jewish father. In short, she is a prototype of the Virgin Mary, who by being immaculately conceived and remaining perpetually chaste, is free of any connection with Jewish patriarchy; and who in her response to the Annunciation became the first Christian.

Shylock, of course, is not really a merchant of Venice, but a moneylender. The merchant who gives the play its title is the equivocal and frequently ignored Antonio. By rereading *The Merchant of Venice* as Antonio's play, Fiedler gives us a character who bears a fascinating resemblance to the speaker in the *Sonnets* and to the even more obscure Antonio of *Twelfth Night.* The character in *Twelfth Night* is a noble sea captain who is identified in the *Dramatis Personae* as "friend to Sebastian." In the course of the play he loses his friend to a beautiful woman and disappears from the action, "struck dumb by a riddle of identity which love itself, not his at any rate, cannot transcend" (*SIS,* 95).

Similarly, the Venetian Antonio loses his young male friend Bassantio to the beautiful Portia, another in Shakespeare's gallery of triumphant transvestites. His devotion to Bassantio is so great that he borrows money to enable his friend to woo Portia and puts up a pound of his own flesh as the security demanded by Shylock. In the comic resolution of the play three young couples are rewarded with marriage, while three older men are frustrated in their deepest desires and thus excluded from the community of bliss that Shakespeare has imagined. Shylock is defeated in court and condemned to become a Christian; Portia's dead father fails to preserve his daughter's virginity when Bassantio foils his riddle of the casks; and Antonio, while gaining both his life and his fortune, is finally more an abandoned father or spurned lover than a successful merchant.

As we have seen from his essay on John Peale Bishop's *Act of Darkness*, Fiedler finds *Othello* to be one of Shakespeare's more mythically resonant plays. In his discussion of that play Fiedler reminds us that the sources from which Shakespeare drew his story did not envision Othello as ethnically black. That particular innovation was Shakespeare's own unique contribution to the fable, and its significance is more symbolic than racial. Shakespeare is not trying to conjure up the Dixonian nightmare of miscegenation (which would have been an historical anachronism in any event), but rather to suggest that Othello is "at the furthest possible cultural remove from the girl he loves and who loves him. . . . It is no mere mistake, however, but the mythmaking instinct of the popular audience which demanded that the destroyer of the most elegant of Patient Griseldas appear in blackface (and she in white, her pallor as much a mask as his swarthiness) in order that they seem as unlike as possible" (*SIS*, 173).

Fiedler suggests that formalistically we should consider *Othello* two plays—a one-act comedy followed by a tragedy in four acts. The comedy ends in typical enough fashion with the young bride escaping her protective father in order to elope with her beloved. In this case, however, the beloved is not Prince Charming but the beast; and the marriage does not bring comic resolution, but provides a bridge to the ensuing tragedy. To complicate matters further, it is a tragedy that comes perilously close to being a bloody farce. Othello (who is mismatched with Desdemona in age as well as race) is busy playing the imagined role of cuckold, while Desdemona is dreaming herself Griselda—the faithful wife whose cruel testing will result in a happy ending.

The figure who orchestrates this tragifarce is Iago, who controls the action from the beginning of act 2 until he is revealed for the devil he is at the midpoint of act 5. During this period of control he plays something very like the Shakespearean fool, accusing Desdemona of faults that the behavior of the other women in the play seems to suggest are common female weaknesses. As fool, he utters generally applicable platitudes which in the particular case of Desdemona prove tragically untrue. Thus, he is less fool than devil, and consequently, morally blacker than Othello. For this reason, Fiedler thinks that Othello should be played by a white man in black face and Iago by a black man in white face. In a film production, the colors could progressively bleach and darken until the two characters had symbolically merged roles by act 3 and reversed them by act 5.

Although there are no Africans or Jews or demonic females in *The Tempest,* Shakespeare's final play exists against a mythic backdrop that makes it, among other things, his definitive statement on the role of the stranger. The magical island on which the action of the play transpires is located on an imaginative continuum that stretches east to Africa and west to America. Although the memory of Africa is understated and the anticipation of America never expressed, both help to define the condition of the European characters who have been removed from more familiar realms of time and space. The two characters who connect us with Africa never appear on stage. One is Claribel, daughter of the king of Naples, who has taken a Tunisian for a husband (at one point the king even sees his present misfortune as a judgment on him for having approved the match). The other is Sycorax, a witch from Algiers who is Caliban's mother. America, on the other hand, is an unspoken presence, the archetypal brave new world that was being settled by Europeans at the time that Shakespeare was writing *The Tempest.*

As we have noted earlier, Fiedler regards Caliban as Shakespeare's image of the New World savage. When that fact is viewed in light of the African roots of his mother, we see a mythic linking of the Negro and the Indian. Caliban (whose name, of course, is an anagram for "cannibal") is the most alien of Shakespeare's strangers because he is a humanoid composite of so many feared outsiders. If Othello's marriage to Desdemona does not quite suggest the horror of miscegenetic rape that has so dominated the Confederate psyche, then Caliban's attempted violation of Miranda clearly does. Should we accept Fiedler's notion that Europeans instinctively view America as a Caliban culture, then it is intriguing to note that Prospero's final reference to Caliban is: "this thing of darkness I / Acknowledge mine." Fiedler sees a "special ambiguity" here. Because the phrase "this thing of darkness I" ends one line of verse, it seems "for a moment completely to identify the occultist Duke with the 'savage and deformed slave'; but it is qualified by the sentence's end, 'acknowledge mine.' Yet there is a ritual ring to the formula, all the same: *'This thing of darkness I / Acknowledge mine,'* as if, through Prospero, all Europe were accepting responsibility for what was to remain forever malign in the America just then being created by conquest and enslavement" (*SIS,* 249).

As with so much of Fiedler's criticism, the idiosyncratic nature of his reading of Shakespeare is designed to produce either squeals of delight or howls of derision (perhaps even both at different times from the same reader). Since an eloquent and compelling defense of this approach was made by Charles Molesworth in his review of *The Stranger in Shakespeare,* I will conclude by quoting him at length:

It was Anatole France, I'm told, who asked the critic to admit, "I'm going to talk about myself apropos of Shakespeare." And who can tell the complete truth when he speaks on that subject? Any sensitive reader feels himself, as he enters those dark places of Cyprus, or Venice or Elsinore, not to mention those darker ones of Othello, Shylock or Hamlet, that he is in many ways an outsider, forced to lie in order to maintain a plausible texture to his presence there. He can construct many alibis for himself, clutch at many partial recognitions, but at bottom he feels as if the places belong to someone else. They do, of course, and this book is a brilliant but refracted glimpse of their proprietor, the only person, perhaps, who was not a stranger to them.[2]

## Chapter Twelve

# Trying His Hand

Like the sportswriter who takes to the athletic field or the political columnist who runs for office, the literary critic who tries his hand at fiction or poetry[1] is courting ridicule. It is perfectly acceptable for an established writer to engage in criticism (just as it is for an ex-jock to become a sportscaster or a retired politician to pontificate on world affairs), because it is presumed that those who can do can also teach. The professional critic, however, is frequently stereotyped as a frustrated artist who spends his time hanging around the literary locker room. At his best, he is an ineffectual Walter Mitty; at his worst, an arrogant phony. That such an outspoken and controversial critic as Leslie Fiedler has published five volumes of fiction therefore evokes the sort of astonishment that Dr. Johnson reserved for women preachers and performing dogs. What is even more impressive than the novelty of his effort is the success with which Fiedler has brought it off.

## Soft Core

"Nobody Ever Died from It" (one of only three stories reprinted in *A Fiedler Reader*) demonstrates its author's ear for dialogue and his gift for humor and characterization. Told by a middle-aged shoe salesman who has always dreamed of being a novelist but who has never published anything, this story recalls a Christmas Eve when the narrator was fourteen and celebrating the holidays with fellow employees of the shoe store where he worked. During the course of the evening, a gallery of grotesque characters reveal their various insecurities under the influence of alcohol and the compulsive merriment of the season. What saves the story from triteness and sentimentality is the obtuseness of the narrator, Hyman Brandler. Because he seems to have no more understanding at thirty-five than he had at fourteen, his consciousness creates an ironic distance between the reader's perception of his story and his own.

The principal character in Brandler's tale is a flagrantly effeminate homosexual named Abie Peckelis (as in peckerless?), who seems to enjoy camping the role of fairy in the shoe store. He is tolerated because of the laughs he provides and the extraordinary number of sales that he makes. Throughout the story he takes young Brandler into his confidence and assumes that the boy's intellectual pretensions make him more sensitive and sympathetic than their fellow workers have proved to be. And yet, at the end of that abbreviated and booze-soaked Christmas Eve, Brandler betrays Abie by joining in the laughter at his friend's expense. (The catalyst is the obvious delight that Abie has shown at being goosed by a policeman's night stick.)

Several of Fiedler's characters, particularly Abie Peckelis, are hilariously well drawn. The ultimate coherence of his story, however, lies in its narrative frame. Although the youthful epiphany recollected from the perspective of one's mature years is a stock theme in literature, Hyman Brandler fails to experience such an epiphany when young, and in his "mature" years compounds his betrayal of Abie by telling his story time and again, whenever there is a lull at a party. Because he makes Brandler a successful storyteller but a failed novelist, Fiedler may be suggesting that human understanding is the quality that separates the true artist from the mere raconteur. As if to emphasize Brandler's continuing lack of this quality, Fiedler ends the story with his narrator's memory (rendered in present tense) of the ridiculous and accusing figure of the fairy: "I smile smugly to myself at the nuttiness of Abie Peckelis—I who at fourteen believe I have never betrayed anything, and know that I never will" (*NC*, 174).

With "Pull Down Vanity!" (first published in *Partisan Review* in 1954), Fiedler begins the exploration of love among the intellectuals that would culminate in his first novel, *The Second Stone* (1963). In writing about a world that he is familiar with Fiedler has the advantage of sounding authentic but the drawback of seeming self-reflexive. In "Pull Down Vanity!" both qualities are evident. The protagonist of this story is a poet named Milton Amsterdam who, during a writer's conference at a Midwestern university, jousts with an old critical nemesis and romances a nubile young secretary. Judging from the title of the story (taken from Pound's *Cantos*) and the various subterfuges in which Amsterdam engages (e.g., he claims to have seven children because he believes it will make him seem more potent), Amsterdam would appear to be something less than a moral norm. And yet, he is admired as an artist and desired as a stud (the only character who is immune to his charms is the aging and despicable critic Edward Fenton).

The major plot conflict develops when Amsterdam becomes involved with an English Department secretary whose husband, an aspiring young working-class poet, has been rendered temporarily impotent by the hostile reaction to his verse. The secretary, Judith Somers, believes that her husband's confidence and sexual prowess will be restored if Amsterdam praises his poetry. While waiting for the therapy to take effect, Judith pursues an affair with Amsterdam. Victimized by the lies he has told about his own potency, Milton cannot perform with Judith when she insists that he use a contraceptive. Thus, when they finally do end up in the sack, their romance remains unconsummated. At the end of a wild and boozy party, Amsterdam confesses his earlier lies, tells some new ones, and leaves in the dawn as Judith and her husband are reunited.

Ultimately, the wit and humor of this story are not sufficient to make it an artistic success. With the exception of the critic Edward Fenton, the characters seem flat and unconvincing (particularly ill-focused is Judith's poet-husband Hank). The narrative is too long and sprawling to work as a short story, but not sufficiently developed to pass as a novella. It is primarily of interest as an apprentice work which introduces themes that will be handled more skillfully in Fiedler's later fiction. A prime example is his notorious tour de force "Nude Croquet."

Originally published in *Esquire* in 1957, this story was frank enough to shock the prudish sensibilities of the age (in addition to being banned in Knoxville, it actually prompted the Du Pont Company to withdraw twelve or fourteen pages of advertising from the magazine). If we regard pornography as the excitement of lust, however, Fiedler's story is decidedly antipornographic. It tells of a party attended by middle-aged intellectuals and artists who have known each other since their impoverished and idealistic youth. Although they have all sold out to success (or made peace with failure), the memory of their early principles leaves them with guilty consciences, and their habit of brutal honesty leads to rancorous confrontations. What we have here is the claustrophobic drama of humiliation-leading-to-insight, the kind of group encounter that Edward Albee so brilliantly depicted in *Who's Afraid of Virginia*

*Woolf?* Because of the concentration achieved by unity of place and time and the richness of Fiedler's controlling metaphor, "Nude Croquet" is a moving and coherent story.

As its title suggests, the climax of the story occurs when the partygoers, far-gone in alcohol and mutual recrimination, decide to cap off the evening with a game of nude croquet. The proposal is made by the young second wife of the host, who sees it as nothing more than an act of zany abandon, à la Scott and Zelda Fitzgerald. For the older guests, however, the stripping of clothes both consummates and exacerbates the stripping of emotions that has been going on all night. As Ronald Bryden observes: "For them it is the necessary continuation of their truthfulness: they will show each other the veined flesh, the sagging bellies and shrunken arms of their dying bodies. Stumbling about by candlelight, in a half-darkness smelling of sweat and age, they perform a ritual reforging of intimacy into melancholy companionship in the face of death."[2]

The game ends when the bitterest of the men (an acerbic Marxist critic and something of a klutz at croquet) falls flat on his face with an apparent heart attack. The lights are switched on, and the young wife who had thought of the entertainment in the first place begins to scream. "One arm concealing her breasts, the other thrust downward so that her hand hid the meeting of her thighs, Molly-o confronted them in the classic pose of nakedness surprised, as if she knew for the first time what it meant to be really nude" (*NC*, 53). Left to ponder this sudden transition from *chutzpah* to *pudeur,* the reader must decide for himself what it means "to be really nude."

Obviously, the mildly decadent frolic that the young woman had had in mind turns into something she had not bargained for. The simulated return to Eden is invariably a mistake for postlapsarian adults. Molly is naive enough to think that such a game can be restricted to fun. What she cannot deal with is the savage honesty that results. Also, as the woman with the most physical attributes and the fewest emotional scars to exhibit, she is flustered when the focus of attention shifts from the physical to the emotional. What she instinctively recoils from displaying is the nakedness of her own innocence. In becoming aware of that innocence, she has taken the first necessary step toward losing it.

Given Fiedler's eminence as a critic and the promise of his early stories, the publication of his first novel—*The Second Stone* (1963)— was something of a literary event. The essential situation it depicts is of a love triangle involving the ultraliberal celebrity rabbi Mark Stone, his boyhood friend Clem Stone (no relation, but more about that later), and Mark's wife Hilda. To heighten the symbolic resonance, the action is played out in Rome (making the novel an "Eastern") during the First International Conference on Love (organized by Mark and financed by a wealthy manufacturer of contraceptives with covert aid from the U.S. State Department) on 30 April–2 May 1953 (a time span that coincides with the Communist celebration of May Day).

By setting *The Second Stone* in Rome, Fiedler calls to mind the long tradition of international or expatriate novels in American literature. What is unclear is whether Fiedler is playing the international theme straight or whether he is writing a parody of the pretentious Eastern. Certainly Rome means different things to different characters. For Clem Stone, expatriation was originally a fashionable gesture against the bourgeois vulgarity of American life. But now, after failing for six years to write his novel, he is no longer an angry young bohemian, but a middle-aged poseur at the end of his tether. Mark, on the other hand, is a successful American "intellectual" who comes to Europe as a consumer of culture (his aging mother and her dentist-fiancé are more conventional tourists seeing the sights). Along with these American characters appears a smattering of anti-American Europeans who make topical references to Eisenhower, Dulles, and the Rosenbergs. And, of course, we have the picturesque ruins of Christian civilization ironically reminding us that we (or at least Fiedler's characters) live in a post-Christian era.

Although the central action of Fiedler's novel involves the competition between Mark and Clem Stone for Hilda's affections, this is only one of several intersecting triangles in *The Second Stone*. For one thing, Clem has a wife back in the United States and vows to return to her because of things he learns about himself in the course of his affair with Hilda (Henry James worked a similar reversal in *The Ambassadors*). Because we know that during his own 1951 pilgrimage to Italy, Fiedler took Hawthorne's *The Marble Faun* along for shipboard reading, the temptation is to fit Hilda and Clem's wife Selma into the dark lady/snow maiden dichotomy. But the question arises as to which is which.

Although Hawthorne's Hilda was a Puritan snow maiden, Clem's *inamorata* is a more ambiguous figure. Early in their relationship, Clem calls her "a snowmaiden disguised as a *femme fatale* disguised as a snowmaiden." And later in the same conversation, he says: "You're not Lady Brett Ashley. You're Daisy Miller, Elsie Dinsmore, Marilyn Monroe" (*SS,* 57). In his discussion of the novel, Samuel Irving Bellman says of Hilda: "Blonde and fair-skinned, she is in one sense an appropriate contrast with the dark complexioned Selma, who in her Semitic origin, her earlier mistreatment of Clem, and her intrinsic vulgarity is fairly well qualified for the position of archetypal Dark Lady. But just as Selma has her contradictory features—she is after all the Good Wife to whom Clem plans to return—Hilda is a bundle of inconsistencies."[3]

There is also a sense in which Hilda is a disruptive force in the lifelong friendship of Clem and Mark. One cannot totally exclude the possibility of a latent Huck-honey relationship between the two.[4] In fact, they seem at times closer than lovers or brothers, more like doppelgängers. Originally, Clem was named Marcus Stone; but to avoid confusion changed his name to Clem, which is short for Clemens, Mark Twain's real name. Thus, Clem is "the other [or second] Mark Stone." Except that Mark's family changed its name from Stein to Stone. So, Clem is actually the *real* Mark (or Marcus) Stone pretending to be Sam Clemens or Mark Twain, suffering from writer's block. At the same time the real Mark Stein is pretending to be Mark Stone or Dr. Kinsey, unwittingly funded by the State Department. (In the midst of this confusion we have Nigger Jim, who pretends to be a black writer named Andrew Littlepage, defecting to the Commies on May Day.)

Just as Walt Whitman, in his poetry, had the disconcerting habit of climbing into bed between honeymooners, so too does Fiedler make his presence felt in this novel. When Clem contemplates writing about his affair with Hilda, the first sentence of his account is the same as the first sentence of *The Second Stone.* Then there is the debate about who actually wrote the avant-garde poem "In Vain From Love's Preakness I Fly." The choices are (1) Mark (under whose name it was published); (2) Clem (who now claims authorship); or (3) a collaboration of the two (which is Mark's present contention). As the cognoscenti know, the answer is (4) none of the above. "In Vain From Love's Preakness I Fly" was published in the July–August 1951 issue of *Partisan Review* under the name Leslie A. Fiedler. And on the whole it is a more satisfying work of art than *The Second Stone.* If Fiedler is correct in saying that the literary pilgrim to Europe must choose "between melodrama and comedy" (*CE,* 1:91), the primary weakness of his first novel is a failure to make that choice, a desire to have it both ways.

## Love and Death in the Rockies

In the early seventies, Fiedler said: "it is a Montana landscape I see when I close my eyes, its people I imagine understanding, or more often misunderstanding me. And in this sense, I have to think of myself as a Western writer."[5] It is in his second novel, *Back to China* (1965), that Fiedler first uses the Montana setting. The contemporary Mountain West serves as time-present, against which is juxtaposed the memory of China immediately after World War II. Fiedler's protagonist, a philosophy professor named Baro Finkelstone, has had himself sterilized as a compulsive act of atonement for the bombing of Hiroshima and spends the next twenty years seeking to maintain his youth by doing dope with his male students and sleeping with his female ones.

Baro (perhaps a pun on "barren") is another one of those rootless Jews who have become fixtures in the contemporary American novel. Fiedler adds an exotic twist, however, by removing this character from a conventional urban environment. The only reminder Baro has of that environment is his left-wing Jewish colleague Hilbert Shapiro. Although the locals have these two confused to the point that they sometimes receive each other's hate mail, Shapiro is a priggish and self-righteous political activist, whereas Finkelstone is an ostensible free spirit. The emnity between the two shows how profoundly Baro is alienated from Jewish stereotypes. Nor does he seem to belong to any alternative culture. When he attends a worship service of the Native American Church, he finds not the ten lost tribes of Israel, but a peyote cult with overtones of fundamentalist Protestant Christianity.

In one sense, Baro is an all-too-familiar figure in American life (and particularly American college life)—the postmenopausal hippie. The only difference is that his vasectomy has brought about an early change of life. Unable to procreate children, he becomes a surrogate father to young bohemians whose ways he apes. Moreover, he is able to copulate at will without fear of the responsibilities of actual paternity. Before his operation he had refrained from interracial sex, even to the point of fleeing an orgy that a Japanese friend had organized for fifty soldiers with fifty geisha girls, but afterward pulls a fat Oriental nurse into bed with him. Not surprisingly, his main playmate in Montana is the Japanese wife of an Indian beatnik he has befriended (the lad dies in a motorcycle wreck before the novel begins). As a kind of pleasure and penance, he pumps his sterile seed into her while looking at two movie stills from *Hiroshima, Mon Amour* tacked to her bedroom door.

If Baro finds sexual ecstasy with a Japanese dark lady, it only stands to reason that he has known frustration with a WASP snow maiden. In this case it is his wife Susannah, an upper-class Episcopalian, whom he has neglected to inform of his operation. Feeling guilty and unfulfilled because of her inability to conceive (there are references to an abortion she has had years earlier), Susannah turns frigid and starts popping tranquilizers and guzzling half-gallon bottles of sherry. One night in a drunken stupor she has either seduced or been seduced by one of Baro's students (presumably her husband was out either dropping acid or getting it on with some third-world lovely). Later that night, she and Baro have one of their infrequent comminglings of the flesh, and she becomes pregnant thinking that the child is his.

If there is something a bit naive about the effort of Faulkner's Ike McCaslin to achieve racial atonement through celibacy, Baro Finkelstone's halfway gesture is downright sophomoric. It is only fitting that this postmenopausal hippie should finally become a "father" through the action of one of his own surrogate children. In a thematically apt, if somewhat contrived, ending, husband and wife become reconciled through this act of infidelity. Baro "remembered his grandfather having told him once that in Jewish law a child begotten by a rapist was considered the child of his mother's husband: a legitimate heir, a true son of Israel, a partaker in the covenant. And he thought, no longer troubled but amused, how among the orthodox, the impotent and sterile must have prayed for a *pogrom,* an assault on their women that would leave them fathers but not cuckolds" (*BC,* 247).

Although it is a moving and engrossing novel, and certainly an improvement over *The Second Stone, Back to China* is not an entirely convincing portrait of reality. It includes too many loose ends, gratuitous characters, and pointless incidents. Moreover, the motivation for the two most important actions in the novel—Baro's vasectomy and his later acceptance of his wife's pregnancy—seem to be ambiguous and arbitrary. It is as if Fiedler gives us too many reasons for the first decision[6] and too few for the second. Nevertheless, he has a genuine feeling for the experience of deracination in the contemporary Mountain West, as is evident in his next major work of fiction—three novellas: "The Last Jew in America," "The Last WASP in the World," and "The First Spade in the West."

This sequence of interrelated narratives is set in the mythical Lewis and Clark City, located somewhere between Montana and Idaho. The first of these concerns itself with the abrasive friendship that unites three old men who were the first twentieth-century Jewish immigrants to settle in the town. One of them is dying in a Catholic hospital, and a second is attempting to persuade the third to help him organize a bedside Yom Kippur service that will include the (largely secularized) Jewish males of the community. Because he has refused to be assimilated into the prevailing WASP culture, Jacob Moskowitz thinks of himself as the last Jew in America. He still speaks with an accent and moves his hands when he talks, but his ethnicity is really a matter of degree. He had lost his religious faith many years before as a boy in Russia (his most vivid memory of his childhood is of his mother's anguished reaction when she caught him deliberately breaking the Yom Kippur fast).

For many years Jacob had devoted himself to the terrestrial faith of communism, but that too proves to be a g—d that failed. Now at seventy, he maintains the cultural trappings of Judaism with the same defiance that had prompted him to repudiate its spiritual substance so many years before. The bedside ritual that he manages to orchestrate turns into something of a farce (his dying friend Louie becomes positively apoplectic when he realizes that there is a crucifix on his wall, and insists that his fellow worshippers wrap it in a towel in the bathroom). And yet, the very fact that the service is well attended suggests something about the residual solidarity of persons who have nothing in common other than their Jewishness, even if they are not quite sure what Jewishness is or means.

On the way out of the hospital, Jacob and his old adversary Max (a successful businessman and other veteran Jew of the community) debate the prospects of an afterlife. To show his disdain for such superstitions, Max sells his share in the hereafter to Jacob for a nickel. Realizing that Max's Catholic wife will insist that he repurchase his piece of eternity, Jacob sits by the phone awaiting Max's call as the story closes. Although Jacob professes to know what Max will want and how he will respond to the request, the

actual conversation is left for us to imagine. As we do so, the biblical
analogue that springs to mind is that of Essau selling his birthright
to his brother Jacob for a mess of pottage. Like the biblical Essau,
Max is a practical man who undervalues spiritual things. And yet,
Jacob Moskowitz was himself referred to as "Essau" when his enraged
mother caught him breaking the Yom Kippur fast. Perhaps Fiedler
sees all contemporary Jewish Americans (even those named Jacob)
as Essau figures, bereft of their birthright and condemned to a
nomadic existence.

Thematically, "The Last WASP in the World" is in many respects
the obverse of "The Last Jew in America." Whereas Jacob Moskowitz
was an Eastern Jew adrift in a WASP West, Vincent Hazelbaker is
a Western WASP immersed in a Jewish East. A native of Lewis
and Clark City, Hazelbaker is a celebrated New York poet whose
wife, two main mistresses, and assorted groupies are all Jewish. The
action of the story takes place on the day and night of the wedding
of his goddaughter (who, according to her mother's insinuations,
is his real daughter as well). Hazelbaker more than lives up to his
reputation as a lush and womanizer, and ends the evening trying
to persuade his three-woman harem to service him simultaneously.
Maintaining a kind of self-protective female camaraderie, they decline and leave him to fantasize about golden Western shikses.

In particular, Vin Hazelbaker remembers a recent trip back to
Lewis and Clark City to give a poetry reading at the local university.
After the session he had been taken by a young professor to a beatnik
coffee house on the site of the old Western bar where he had had
his first sexual experience many years before. (The girl was a young
Indian whore named the Princess, a kind of demythologized Saca-
jawea whom he remembers having done for him "what no one
afterward would ever do for him worse.")[7] There, he is picked up
by a Jewish coed who walks him back to his motel and stays for a
quick tumble in bed. The girl he really remembers from that evening, however, was a pale WASP student who praised his rather
pedestrian poetry reading and who reminded him of the girl he
sought everywhere—"a friend, a compatriot, a relative, among the
alien heads of the darker, more vivid types who clustered to hear
him. . . . He would never sleep with such girls, feeling himself
in relation to them a father, a priest, a ministering angel in a dream"
(*LJ*, 107).

We have here, of course, the old dichotomy of snow maiden and dark lady. The latter female exists for sex, the former for worship. Having become satiated with sex, the romantic Hazelbaker still dreams of the pure, ethereal, unattainable Western girl. For him this figure has become epitomized by Ardith Eugenia Sparrow, the young woman he had met in Lewis and Clark City. Early in the story we learn that Vin is distressed by a letter he has received from Miss Sparrow; however, Fiedler witholds the contents of that letter from us until the very end. It is then that we discover that the pale, chaste, WASP goddess has expressed her desire for the poet in the crassest terms possible. Disillusioned and drunk, Vincent Hazelbaker lies in bed, with a phone in his hand but no number to dial, and a cry for help on his lips.

Although the West may simply be an alien environment in "The Last Jew in America" and an elusive dream in "The Last WASP in the World," it is the essential thematic landscape of "The First Spade in the West." (To varying degrees, all four myths of the West identified in *The Return of the Vanishing American* are travestied in this novella.) If Fiedler is trying to say that the utopian West is quite literally nowhere, then it is appropriate that this most western of his fictions focus on that ultimately displaced person the American Negro. Fiedler's Ned York is descended from the black guide who accompanied Lewis and Clark, owns his own cocktail lounge in Lewis and Clark City, and hopes to impress his children by being named Kiwanis Man of the Year. When he occasionally entertains his customers with a rendition of "When I Was a Cowboy," they think that it is a novelty; however, Ned realizes that the song belongs to no white artist, but to the legendary black folksinger Leadbelly.

In terms of our basic racial stereotypes, any successful black businessman is a source of irony (this is the basic premise behind the long-running television sitcom *The Jeffersons*). In the course of Fiedler's narrative, we see Ned arguing politics with a liberal hippie who is the leader of his house band, currying favor with the richest white lady in town, and ejecting a disreputable Indian slut from his bar. The latter character is what Vincent Hazelbaker's first love the Princess has become—the anti-Pocahontas who is a stock figure of the New Western. (In her various guises, this figure is simply "a whore begging to be screwed. . . , growing fatter and fatter, as well as ever more slatternly and insatiable" [R, 153].) By the same token, Hannah Duston, the female scourge of dark-skinned

savages, has been transformed into Ned's ex-wife, a white woman
who has married yet another black man (to serve as surrogate father
to her mixed-blood children) and is constantly hitting Ned up for
money to get this worthless new husband out of scrapes. Or perhaps
she is only a white pseudo-Pocahontas demonstrating the impos-
sibility of redemptive interracial love.

After a night of hard drinking, the aging matriarch of the town
and her gigolo boyfriend (secretly her new husband) are too soused
to drive back to their cabin in the mountains. Ned chauffers them
home and is drafted into hauling the old crone's ashes while her
husband is passed out on the living room floor. The experience
proves too much for the bride who dies of a heart attack. Fortunately,
the cuckold's homosexual boyfriend (Ned's bandleader) shows up
and helps Ned dump the husband's comatose body in the nuptial
bed. The novella closes with the gaudy public funeral of Mrs. Elmira
Gallagher, complete with "traditional" western honor guard: "There
they were," Fiedler writes, "in full cowboy outfits, all four of them,
because that was the way Elmira had wanted it: chaps and bandanas,
high-heel boots and spurs, and a ten gallon hat on the chair right
behind each of them, the works. . . . Standing there dressed like
cowpokes [were] a beatnik from the East, a little sheeny with a shoe
clerk's mustache, a big fat queer who'd struck it rich, and a spade"
(*LJ*, 190–91).

Lewis and Clark City obviously exists on what Fiedler has called
the "third frontier," where pop images of the West are not only
exploited for profit but have become a kind of ersatz reality. Since
the pop West is a product of invention, there is theoretically no
reason why the four improbable members of Mrs. Gallagher's honor
guard should not pose as cowboys. Indeed, this closing scene is
simply the most obvious and most elaborate of the many parodies
to be found in "The First Spade in the West." In the bedroom tryst
of Ned and Mrs. Gallagher we have an hilarious inversion of *southern*
obsessions. Instead of the black man raping the white woman, we
have the white woman seducing the black man. There is even an
echo of Thomas Dixon, Jr., in Elmira Gallagher's telling Ned that
when she was a child "they taught us girls to be scairt of negras
like they was some kind of wild animal like a gorilla or something"
(*LJ*, 160). Then, we have the obvious reversal of gender roles when
the old woman dies from a too strenuous sexual encounter with a
younger man.

However, the central western myth of interethnic male bonding is strangely absent from this story. Mrs. Gallagher's widower and his boy friend manage to escape from petticoat government along with the old woman's money; but these two are of the same ethnic extraction, live in civilization, and serve as comic figures, not as moral norms. Moreover, Ned York is no Nigger Jim or Chingachgook, but an honorary white man who has sold out to the dream of bourgeois success. From a mythic standpoint, then, "The First Spade in the West" is most significant for what it fails to depict. It is not even a straightforwardly antimythic tale. Fiedler seems to be saying that the old myths are now so dead that even in satire they can be evoked only obliquely.

## Yin and Yang

In *What Was Literature?*, Fiedler notes: "I had long read futurist fantasy, but only since realizing its connections with our chiliastic view of history have I explored it in depth. . . . Imagining the future . . . is for me finally just another way of discovering or inventing a usable past" (*WWL*, 16, 17). This is certainly true of his one published science fiction novel *The Messengers Will Come No More*. As he has said of science fiction in general, this novel essentially consists of dreams masquerading as extrapolations. Set in the twenty-sixth century, the narrative postulates a future in which the present inchoate feminist revolution has achieved total supremacy. With black women at the top of a racist, sexist social hierarchy, we have a variation on that old cliché of satire—inversion of the familiar.

This future matriarchy assigns to men the same role that women have traditionally occupied in fundamentalist Islamic countries, that of sexual slave. Fiedler's protagonist—a Jewish archaeologist and scribe named Jacob—has been the obedient stud of two women during his life. However, both Marcia and Megan have "expelled" (i.e., divorced) him for various reasons (the latter because he surreptitiously had their son circumcised). He is now making time with a young polymorphous nymph named Melissa-Melinda (not as high on the social register as Marcia or Megan, Melissa-Melinda resembles a lame-brained hippie of 1960s vintage). Not only do all of the women in Jacob's neck of the woods have names that begin with "M," but Melissa-Melinda is a double "M," like that mid-twentieth-century goddess Marilyn Monroe. And just so we do not miss the point, Fiedler invokes Marilyn's divine name about two thirds of the way through the novel. Here, he describes the final death throes of Gutenberg culture: "It began with the firing of the Library at the Marilyn Monroe School of Women's Studies (formerly Yale University) by an Assistant Professor of Witchcraft. Refused tenure for her failure to 'publish,' she first kindled the flames, then flung herself into them from the rooftop solarium of the 125-story Parapsychology Building. In the next few days, her example was followed by hundreds, thousands, finally tens of thousands of her colleagues in all lands, who combined book-burning with suicide— not singly, as in the first instance, but in groups of twenty or more" (M, 149–50).

The usable past that Fiedler derives from this bizarre vision of the future is a radical reinterpretation of the life of Jesus. Because of his arcane knowledge of the long-dead Hebrew language, Jacob is entrusted with the task of translating some ancient scrolls that fit Jesus and the Virgin Mary into a Yin-Yang conflict which has bedeviled Judaism at least since the power struggle between Mary's namesake Miriam and her brother Moses (the golden calf of the wilderness being only one of many pagan female deities to challenge the patriarchal faith of the Jews). In this rewriting of scripture, Jesus is not divinely conceived by the power of the Holy Ghost, but is a product of the Blessed Virgin's liaison with an extraterrestrial "Messenger." This being later spirits the crucified Lord's soul into the heavens, where it will presumably participate in some inter-galactic war of the sexes.

The outer-space angle gives something of a new twist to the otherwise conventional motif of the Passover Plot. What is unique is Fiedler's demythologizing of the Virgin Mary. In his version, the girl starts out determined to be a prophetess rather than a traditional wife. In order to maintain her virginity, she contracts a nominal marriage with an impotent old carpenter who has been cuckolded by a succession of previous wives. When she does conceive, with maidenhead intact, she soon becomes the ultimate Jewish mother ("My Son, the Messiah") who raises up a rival to the faith of her fathers. The final irony is that she herself becomes a quasi-goddess figure in the new Christian religion.

This novel is promising in concept, but disappointing in exe-cution. In the futuristic sequences, one is never really sure whether

Fiedler is warning us against the dangers of feminism or is using the turnabout theme as a way of condemning sexism in general. If he is simply trying to be entertaining rather than profound, the joke goes on for too long. The Jesus story gives Fiedler the opportunity to write an historical novel of ideas. Instead, he settles for a spoof of exegetical pedantry. Throughout, his compulsive vulgarity seems to exist only for its own sake and sheds no real light on the interaction of the sacred and the profane. For this reason, it is not so much sacrilegious as trivial. Fiedler calls *The Messengers Will Come No More* "the most unread of all my work" (*WWL,* 16–17). It is doubtful that his reputation will suffer for its remaining so.

## Chapter Thirteen
# Outside Literature

Although Fiedler's critics have justly chastised him for his vices, what they have found particularly unforgivable are his virtues. One of the most conspicuous of those is an eclecticism that is constantly taking him outside the realm of pure exegesis. Formalist critics think him too sociological, and sociologists think him too literary. (Those of us who are hesitant to separate the various aspects of culture into tidy little pigeonholes tend to approve of his method while occasionally disagreeing with his specific conclusions.) Typical of this anti-eclectic bias are the comments of Richard Chase on *Love and Death in the American Novel.* "Indicting a culture in terms of its literature and in the guise of a literary critic is a not too happy expedient," Chase writes. "Ideally [Fiedler] should have written two books—in one of which he could have been preponderantly the cultural analyst and prophet and in the other preponderantly the literary historian and critic. Matthew Arnold's *Culture and Anarchy* is one thing, his *Essays in Criticism* another."[1] While it is true that Fiedler has never adhered rigidly to the Arnoldian distinction, we can classify many of his works as more or less literary than others. Thus, in a study concerned primarily with Fiedler's *Essays in Criticism,* it may not be amiss to devote a single chapter to his *Culture and Anarchy.*

## From Dreams Awake

As a self-proclaimed cultural barbarian who has praised the sixties' counterculture and whose greatest notoriety was the result of a drug bust, Fiedler would seem to be the sort of pinko liberal professor whom no self-respecting conservative father would want his daughter (or even his son) to take a course from. And yet, the opening entries in his first collection of essays—*An End to Innocence*—are powerfully articulate indictments of the liberal response to three of the most galvanizing political issues of the late forties and early fifties: the Hiss case, the Rosenberg trial, and McCarthyism. As Ronald Bryden has said in comparing Fiedler to *Mary* McCarthy: "Where she exposes the logical contradictions to which liberal idealism lies open if pressed to conclusions, he attacks it at the point where it achieves single-minded logic by turning its back on the rich contradictoriness of reality."[2]

As the title of Alistair Cooke's study of the Hiss case suggests, in that particular controversy an entire generation was on trial. This was the generation of American liberals and fellow travelers who saw in the Soviet Union only an ally against fascism. This myth was particularly prevalent during the thirties, when the Spanish Civil War fired the imagination of the left, and was reestablished when the Americans and Soviets joined forces in World War II. Although few people committed espionage, many who flirted with communism felt themselves capable of having done so had the opportunity presented itself. They would not have considered such an act treason against their country, but rather loyalty to the more abstract cause of progress and humanity. To proclaim Hiss innocent was to say that, even if he did steal sensitive government documents, his motives were pure, because no deed committed on behalf of the left could be fundamentally evil.

Fiedler found Alger Hiss to be the epitome of the Popular Front Bolshevik—a Communist whose very usefulness to the Party lay in appearing to be everything that that party theoretically hated. He was an establishment American of impeccable credentials—law clerk to Justice Holmes, aide to President Roosevelt, highly placed State Department official, and later president of the Carnegie Endowment for World Peace. His accuser, on the other hand, was a throwback to an earlier period of party history—the obsessive poet-bum, a Dostoyevskian underground man. Appearances were all on Hiss's side (so much so that Secretary of State Dean Acheson's investigation of rumors about Hiss's Communist ties consisted of asking Alger's brother Donald if the charges were true; "after all, he had known 'the Hiss boys' since they were children" [*CE,* 1:22]). All that Whittaker Chambers had going for him was the fact that he was telling the truth.

Alger Hiss portrayed himself as having been victimized by false charges, but the evidence of his guilt was so overwhelming that this stubborn insistence on his "innocence" finally deprived Hiss of the tragic dignity that might have earned him a measure of respect, rather than the pity and contempt he so richly deserved. "If there is a note of tragedy in the case," Fiedler writes, "it is provided by Chambers, the informer driven to mortify himself and to harm those he still loved. The Third Perioder, still pursuing the absolute, makes a tragic final appearance as the scorned squealer; the Popular Fronter can only exist in the role of the hopeless liar" (*CE*, 1:23).

What is most significant about the Hiss case is not the behavior of its principals, as historically revealing and intensely dramatic as that was, nor even the impetus that it gave directly to the career of Richard Nixon and indirectly to that of Joe McCarthy. Rather, the Hiss case will be remembered as a watershed in liberalism's long struggle for (or perhaps against) maturity. "American liberalism has been reluctant to leave the garden of its illusion," Fiedler writes; "but it can dally no longer: the age of innocence is dead. The Hiss case marks the death of an era, but it also promises a rebirth if we are willing to learn its lessons." The primary lesson, of course, is that there is evil on the left as well as the right; that "there is no magic in the words 'left' or 'progressive' or 'socialist' that can prevent deceit and the abuse of power." Finally, Fiedler leaves us with a warning: "without the understanding of what the Hiss case tries desperately to declare, we will not be able to move forward from a liberalism of innocence to a liberalism of responsibility" (*CE*, 1:24).

An even more spectacular spy case, one that stirred international passion in a way that the Hiss melodrama failed to do, was that of Julius and Ethel Rosenberg—two American Communists whose espionage activities enabled the Soviets to construct an atomic bomb. For the die-hard left, the Rosenbergs (or rather a contrived image of them) have remained martyrs to the "witch hunt" mentality of the fifties. They have also been eulogized in numerous works of literature, the most distinguished of which are E. L. Doctorow's *The Book of Daniel* and Robert Coover's *The Public Burning*. As Fiedler noted in the October 1953 issue of *Encounter*, there are really two Rosenberg cases—the actual one tried in a court of law and the symbolic one that continues to be argued in the court of ideology. It is because these two very different cases are referred to by the same name that it is difficult to talk sense about them.

The legal case against the Rosenbergs is easier to discuss because it is the more tangible of the two. Like Alger Hiss, the Rosenbergs steadfastly maintained their innocence in the face of overwhelming evidence to the contrary. Fiedler suspects that this is once again a shorthand way of saying: whatever I may have done was justified by a higher loyalty. Since the United States had already used the atomic bomb and the virtuous Soviets would never do so, giving them the secret of the bomb would maintain a balance of power that would insure world peace. If this is what the Rosenbergs actually believed, they should have said so rather than proclaiming an innocence which, because it was so demonstrably false, dehumanized them almost as much as their prior act of treason.

Just as establishment New Deal types such as Dean Acheson were reluctant to see the truth about Alger Hiss, so too were American radicals and fellow travelers incapable of admitting that the Rosenbergs were guilty (the Communists, who knew the truth, simply exploited the situation and sacrificed the Rosenbergs for their own strategic ends). By becoming symbols for their attackers and defenders, and ultimately even for themselves, the Rosenbergs ceased to exist as human beings. For this very reason, Fiedler argues, the Rosenbergs should have been spared.

When the humanity of the Rosenbergs was denied by their comrades and by themselves, the burden of its defense was left with us. While it is true that our execution of two guilty people pales when compared to the Soviet "execution" of millions of innocent ones, a commutation for the Rosenbergs would have been an even higher road for us to take. "Before the eyes of the world we lost an opportunity concretely to assert what all our abstract declarations can never prove: that for us at least the suffering person is realer than the political moment that produces him or the political philosophy for which he stands" (*CE*, 1:45).

If the Hiss case raised the specter of Soviet infiltration of the U.S. government, the exposure of the Rosenbergs reminded Americans of what was at stake. As the technological sophistication of warfare increased exponentially with the development of nuclear weapons, the cost of espionage became correspondingly greater. This fact put the Democrats, who had originally protected Hiss, on the defensive and gave the hapless Republicans their first real issue in twenty years. It also stirred a kind of populist resentment among middle Americans who may have liked Roosevelt but who detested the liberal bluebloods and eggheads that he had brought into the government. All that was lacking was a right-wing demagogue opportunistic enough to take advantage of the situation. That vacuum was filled when, at 8:00 P.M. on 9 February 1950, the junior senator from Wisconsin told the Women's Republican Club of Wheeling,

West Virginia, that he knew of 205 Communists in the State Department. Joe McCarthy was a historical inevitability.

Like Alger Hiss and the Rosenbergs, McCarthy played both a practical and a symbolic role in American life; or rather two symbolic roles. Fiedler makes this point when he asks us to "choose a passerby at random in any of the great cities of the world and ask him to identify the 'X' in the following quotation: 'Beware, Commies, spies, traitors, and foreign agents! X, with all loyal, free men behind him, is looking for you, ready to fight until the last one of you is exposed for the yellow scum you are!' "

" 'McCarthy,' he will tell you, 'Joe McCarthy, of course,' though he might be incapable of saying whether the actual lines were a publicity release from McCarthy's supporters or a parody of such a release by his worst enemies. Actually, the name for which I have substituted an 'X' is 'Captain America,' and the warning is taken from a comic book for small boys. But the implied commentary is apt: in our world, what seems to one group a howling travesty strikes another as a clarion call to action; and a legend has become confused with a man" (*CE*, 1:46). The purpose of Fiedler's essay is to dispel that confusion.

Given the enthusiasm (some would say hysteria) of both the pro- and anti-McCarthy forces, Fiedler was challenging the conventional wisdom in suggesting that the senator was neither a knight on a white horse nor a homegrown Hitler, but a depressingly ordinary and venal politician who was much smaller than the controversies in which he was embroiled. Similarly, those who supported and those who attacked him frequently did so for self-serving reasons— the former out of cultural or partisan animus toward his targets, the latter out of a desire to discredit the entire anti-Communist movement. McCarthy was finally brought down not because of the harm he was doing to civil liberties or to the fight against communism, however, but because his idiosyncratic hostility toward the Army caused him seriously to misplay his hand.

The one thing about which the liberal mythology is most certain is that McCarthy and McCarthyism brought a temporary halt to free speech in America. The truth is that, although some innocent people did suffer during the McCarthy era, the vast majority who attacked the senator and his methods did so with impunity. Indeed, in intellectual circles, the only people who were likely to experience ostracism were those who supported McCarthy. Fiedler sets the record straight on this point without arguing (as William Buckley does) that the intemperance of McCarthy's enemies somehow vindicated the senator himself. I suspect that Fiedler's opinion would be closer to that of Peter Vierick—that the Communist cause was served by both Owen Lattimore and Joseph McCarthy: Lattimore "by the way he defended it," and McCarthy "by the way he attacks it."[3]

## Tear Down the Walls

Because most of us who are familiar with Leslie Fiedler know him through his books and articles or his public lectures, we are apt to forget that all of these activities are performed within the context of his role as a professional academic. Fiedler has not only been an outstanding (and controversial) university professor, but he has also pondered the nature of the vocation he is pursuing. Like so many critics of education, Fiedler wishes to advance what he regards as the primary obligations of the university by protecting it from extraneous demands on its resources and its loyalty. These issues are most fully discussed in "The Crumbling Ivory Tower" and "Academic Irresponsibility."

The first of these essays—preserved in Fiedler and Jacob Vincour's *The Continuing Debate* (1964)—makes the familiar traditionalist argument that the "service" function of the university (i.e., providing the public with everything from football games to luncheon addresses) should not be allowed to subvert its more fundamental obligation to be a place of free intellectual inquiry. In addition to the compromises that the university must make with those who are footing the bill (e.g., taxpayers or alumni) some purely internal conditions also militate against the educational process. These include the arbitrary division of classes into fifty-minute periods that are begun and ended by the ringing of a Pavlovian bell, narrow academic specialization, and the power of technocratic administrators who neither understand nor respect the humanistic tradition of the academy. Except for his endorsement of greater social freedom for students, there is little in Fiedler's essay that might alarm a modern-day Matthew Arnold or John Henry Newman.

By the time we get to "Academic Irresponsibility," however, the situation has changed. The year is 1968 and the always difficult relations between the university and the rest of society have reached the point of (sometimes violent) polarization. For years those on the gown side of the town-gown controversy had included in their defense of academic freedom a ritualistic acknowledgment of something called "academic responsibility." In practical terms, what this meant was that political dissidents would be protected but advocates of hallucinogenic drugs or promiscuous sex would be thrown to the wolves. Fiedler dissents from that compromise position by arguing that freedom of thought and expression, if it is to have any meaning, must be absolute. The only "responsibility" that such freedom entails is the willingness to defend the intellectual cogency of one's position and to remain open to new evidence and to differing points of view.

Fiedler's extreme libertarianism and open-mindedness puts him at odds with authoritarians of both the left and the right, with Herbert Marcuse and William Buckley. Simply put, the authoritarian view holds that the purpose of education is to promulgate truth and that that purpose is thwarted when we treat all ideas as equal. The notion that truth will always defeat error in a free and open contest is a sentimental canard that is contradicted by the bitter lessons of history. (The authoritarian mentality caused influential right-wingers to try to purge leftist professors in the fifties and radical students to shout down conservative speakers in the sixties.)

The libertarian, however, tends to find "truth" to be more elusive and to regard most questions of values to be still theoretically open. Fiedler puts the issue very succinctly when he says: "If any kind of truth or pursuit of truth—however misguided, however wrong— seems threatening to a cause we espouse, it is time to reexamine that cause, no matter how impressive its credentials" (CE, 2:373). True to his principles, Fiedler has always criticized attempts to suppress points of view with which he disagrees. He writes, for example, that "Surely one of the most scandalous events of recent academic history has been the quiet dismissal of a distinguished rightist teacher of political science from an equally distinguished Ivy League college, whose own silence was bought by buying up his contract and whose colleagues' silence apparently did not have to be bought at all" (CE, 2:371–72).[4]

What Fiedler fails to do is to answer the question that William Buckley posed in *God and Man at Yale* and that the American public began to ask during the upheavals of the sixties: does a society have an obligation to finance institutions that are contemptuous of that society's basic values? Unless that question can be answered, "universities" will increasingly come to resemble postsecondary centers for job training, while the traditional liberal arts curriculum goes the way of opera and ballet—an elitist activity enjoyed by the cultured few and shunned by the masses. I suspect that Fiedler's recent efforts toward crossing the border and closing the gap between canonical and popular literature is at least in part a constructive reaction to the loss of public confidence in the humanities.

## Defining the Human

In the spring of 1978 Fiedler was back on the talk show circuit, not as a celebrity nut defending the freaked-out youth of America, but as a respected authority on popular culture pushing his latest book—a meditation on human oddities entitled, appropriately enough, *Freaks: Myths and Images of the Secret Self.* It was a book "so equivocally 'interdisciplinary' that library catalogers did not know whether to classify it under 'psychology,' 'sociology,' or 'literary criticism.' " "Actually," Fiedler tells us, "my model for it (a secret guessed by one acute reviewer)[5] was Richard Burton's *Anatomy of Melancholy,* which would make it, I guess, what used to be called belles lettres; though it has, in fact, intrigued chiefly 'soft' and semi-'soft' scientists, longing to rejoin the humanities" (*WWL,* 34–35). The thesis of this book is that genetic mutants reveal to "normal" people many of their hidden dreams and nightmares. Once again, Fiedler is defining the human in terms of the marginal rather than the central.

Fiedler begins his discussion by looking at freaks of scale (dwarfs and giants). These are by far the most common human curiosities and the ones who most frequently inhabit our myths and dreams. Of the two, dwarfs have historically been the most favored. From the time of Knoumhopou, a dwarf who served as keeper of the royal wardrobe in ancient Egypt, until well into the eighteenth century, dwarfs were court favorites who served as royal advisers (Fiedler even notes that a few dwarf warriors—Charles III of Naples and Sicily, Ladislas I of Poland, and, according to some accounts, even Attila the Hun—"have proved themselves as capable of leading their people in battle as any six-foot-tall king" [*F,* 60]). By the late nineteenth century, however, dwarfs had become simply objects of pity and wonder, rather than of veneration. In our own time, they have been exhibited by P. T. Barnum, murdered by Adolf Hitler (who saw them as affronts to the eugenic purity of the master race), and eventually transformed from religious marvel to medical patient to oppressed minority.

If dwarfs (and the host of other little people who have been known by various literary and medical names) are among the most loved of freaks, giants are among the most feared. The reason for this may be no more sinister than the fact that at one time we were all Gullivers in a world of Brobdingnagians, whereas very few can empathize with the plight of the overgrown. When giants appear in our folklore, whether it be the biblical Goliath or the ogre of *Jack and the Beanstalk,* it is usually as foil to a smaller but more cunning opponent. In reading these stories we may simply be indulging fantasies of patricide, an explanation that takes on even more interesting Freudian implications when we consider that the hero is frequently assisted by the giant's treacherous wife.

Although they may not be freaks of scale in quite the same sense as dwarfs and giants, excessively fat and excessively thin people have long been featured in side shows and celebrated in popular legends. At a deep psychological level, the obese (particularly obese women) represent the dream of eros, while human skeletons signify the fear of thanatos: "All of us have memories of having once been cuddled against the buxom breast and folded into the ample arms of a warm, soft Giantess, whose bulk—to our 8-pound, 21-inch infant selves— must have seemed as mountainous as any 600-pound Fat Lady to our adult selves" (F, 131). In contrast, the hideously emaciated do not challenge our "conventional notions about growing up or growing down. Rather, they call into question the distinction between the living and the dead" (F, 134).

The distinction called into question by hermaphrodites is, of course, the one between male and female. When the pagan notion of divine androgyny gave way to the patriarchal myths of Judaism and Christianity, the hermaphrodite became a monster to be shunned or an oddity to be exploited. Only in recent years, with the demise of Judaism and Christianity and the rise of a kind of neo-paganism, has the situation changed. The unisex look in fashion has tended to blur traditional gender identity; radical feminists are attacking the rigidity of sex roles for political reasons; and transsexuals are increasingly going under the knife to conform their outward appearance to their psychic orientation. The cumulative result of these developments has been to "normalize" what previous ages have either revered or repudiated as abnormal.

For Fiedler, the ultimate freaks are Siamese Twins (and the even more hideous autosite-parasite linkages). These call into question the distinction between self and other: "Standing before Siamese Twins, the beholder sees them looking not at each other, but—both at once—at him. And for an instant it may seem to him that he is a third brother, bound to the pair before him by an invisible bond; so that the distinction between audience and exhibit, we and them, normal and Freak, is revealed as an illusion, desperately, perhaps even necessarily, defended, but untenable in the end" (*F, 36*). Because medical science is making the separation of Siamese Twins an increasingly common occurrence, this type of freak is rapidly becoming obsolescent. Instead of being of central importance themselves, they "have become supernumeraries in a psychodrama starring the doctors who make normal humans out of monsters" (*F, 199*).

Having introduced the reader to an entire gallery of human oddities, Fiedler turns his attention to the image of the freak in modern culture. Although his discussion here leads to repetition of some points made earlier, it is the most valuable part of his book, elevating the entire study from the level of mere sensationalism. Of particular interest is his suggestive examination of the relationship between freak shows and horror literature. Both are fundamentally forms of pornography designed to excite an uncontrollable reaction, in this case not an erection but a shudder. It is therefore not surprising that from the time of Mary Shelley's *Frankenstein* and Bram Stoker's *Dracula* in the early nineteenth century until the present, the human mutant has become a stock figure of horror literature. How appropriate that a single film director—Tod Browning—should have been responsible for the horror classic *Dracula* (1931) and the hauntingly grotesque *Freaks* (1932).

Although *Dracula* has remained consistently popular, *Freaks* was so far ahead of its time that it was greeted with initially hostile reviews and had to be revived, three decades after its release, as an underground cult film. Browning takes us beyond the exhibitionism of the carnival to show us human oddities as flesh-and-blood people with their own lives and their own sense of community. Indeed, our sympathies are so much with the freaks that they seem more truly human than their "normal" adversaries. An unabashed popular-izer, Browning managed to create a mythically resonant work of high art. Unfortunately, as Fiedler points out, a gratuitously "mag-ical" ending partially undercuts the realism upon which the delicate empathy of audience for artifact has been based.

Science fiction, which is sometimes indistinguishable from horror literature, has also exploited what Fiedler calls "the myth of the mutant." The stories in Isaac Asimov's *I Robot*, for example, depict robots striving to be accepted as men, just as Frankenstein's monster had done in Mary Shelley's immortal novel a century before. Even more moving to the counterculture are tales of men mutating rather than manufacturing themselves into metahumans—novels such as A. E. Van Vogt's *Slan*, Arthur C. Clarke's *Childhood's End*, and Robert A. Heinlein's *A Stranger in a Strange Land*. These works challenge the boundaries between the human and the nonhuman just as profoundly as the Elephant Man and the Dog-faced Boy once did, stirring "similar feelings of sacrilege and terror" (*F*, 321).

As engrossing as this book is, it is not without flaws. For one thing, it could have used a more detailed discussion of P. T. Barnum. Fiedler describes Barnum as "a mass educator as well as a mass entertainer, and finally a magician able—long after science thought it had neutralized nature—to remythify it by reviving in adults the awe children feel before its variety and abundance" (*F*, 279). This interpretation is so much at odds with the standard view of Barnum as merely a cynical bunkum artist that one is left begging for elaboration that is never adequately supplied.

Another surprising omission is Fiedler's failure to mention James Thurber's classic short story "You Could Look It Up" in his dis-cussion of freaks in literature (or even to list that story in his bibliography).[6] This tale of a midget who is sent up to pinch hit in a major league baseball game raises in a humorous context the whole issue of human scale (given the proliferation of low-brow sports literature for boys, there probably are plenty of stories of giants in basketball as well). Not only is Thurber's tale a staple of short story anthologies, but it inspired Bill Veeck (the P. T. Barnum of professional sports) to sign a midget to play with the old St. Louis Browns. When that midget actually did pinch hit and drew a walk, there was such an outcry that little people were officially banned from the game. This bizarre chain of events raises the specter of life imitating art and also reminds us that there are certain areas of human endeavor where freaks may actually have an advantage over their "normal" counterparts.

The most problematic aspect of Fiedler's study is his attempt to draw a connection between yesterday's circus freaks and today's drug freaks. That the term *freak* is used by the psychedelic young is simply an example of their proudly appropriating a term of derision (sort of like blacks calling themselves "niggers" or homosexuals referring to themselves as "queers"). The main difference between genetic curiosities and hippies (and this is so obvious that one almost hesitates to mention it) is that the latter have chosen their condition, while the former have not. To be abnormal by choice is, at best, a form of slumming that lacks even the misguided nobility shown by the young upper-class liberal who takes a job in a factory or as a migrant worker. Rather than dwelling on the counterculture (how dated that now seems), Fiedler would have been better advised to give some consideration to freaks as human beings. One need not be a maudlin sentimentalist to believe that such a strategy would have provided balance to Fiedler's view of freaks as mythic icons. There are moments in Tod Browning's movie that cause us to feel the tenuousness of our traditional concepts of normality. In Fiedler's book, that tenuousness is frequently postulated but never felt.

## Chapter Fourteen
# The Critic Who Made Us

When I began to study modern literary criticism in the early 1970s, there seemed to be a consensus (at least insofar as such things are reflected in standard textbooks) that there were no more than half a dozen approaches worth examining in depth.[1] These were the formalist (mostly "new critical" and neo-Aristotelian), moral (mostly neo-humanist), sociological (mostly Marxist), psychological (mostly Freudian), and archetypal (mostly Jungian). Of these, the neo-Aristotelian, neo-humanist, and Marxist schools were considered to be primarily of historical interest. Thus, a practicing critic could learn his craft from relatively few masters and devote the lion's share of his energy to reading the primary texts themselves. Over the next decade or so, the situation was to change radically.

To begin with, the social approach made a strong comeback from both the feminist left and the neo-conservative right. Also, theological criticism (an interesting hybrid of the archetypal and moral) has gained a certain prominence.[2] But, most important, the thought of such European figures as Roland Barthes and Jacques Derrida has given rise to an entirely new discipline called "critical theory." The difference between "critical theory" and the more traditional approaches, it seems to me, is greater than that which separates any of the traditional approaches from each other. The avant-garde theoreticians (be they structuralists, deconstructionists, or whatever) speak in a jargon that often seems better suited to the more esoteric reaches of philosophy than to literary exegesis. One reads their convoluted syntax hoping that there is more there than meets the eye, but fearing that there is less. In any event, literary criticism has been transformed from a vehicle for understanding literature (a noble enough aspiration in the era of Brooks and Warren) to being almost an end in itself.

Within the new scheme of things, even such an iconoclastic critic as Leslie Fiedler becomes something of a traditionalist. Although some may find his methods and conclusions to be questionable, he shares at least two basic assumptions with virtually all traditional critics: he believes that literature is of central importance to life and that by shedding light on literature the critic can help to clarify that importance for his readers. (In 1982, Fiedler told Patricia Ward Biederman: "I want to write as differently as possible from structuralist, post-structuralist, deconstructionist critics who write a private jargon, a secret language, hermetic code that's only available to the initiated.")[3] Although he is usually regarded as a Jungian myth critic, Fiedler has not hesitated to borrow the insights of Marx and Freud when they seemed relevant to his task. Moreover, "No! In Thunder" is a classic example of moral criticism, and "Dante: Green Thoughts in a Green Shade" of close reading and formal analysis. Like all decent critics, Fiedler is capable of creative eclecticism.

What distinguishes him from many of his fellow traditionalists, as well as from the critical theory crowd, is his sustained effort to reach an audience outside the academy. As one might expect, this has caused him to be scorned in some circles as a shallow popularizer and showboat. A more charitable, and I think more accurate, characterization would be to see him as part of what is left of a once-flourishing species—the man of letters. The first generation or two of modern critics consisted largely of nonacademic types who "prided themselves on being amateurs, dilettantes; or if professionals at all, journalists, book reviewers and especially contributors to, founders and editors of 'little magazines,' adversary literary quarterlies" (*WWL*, 59). Although such individuals may have made periodic forays into the classroom, it was with the same casualness as today's novelist or poet-in-residence. Unlike lesser mortals, they were not expected to teach freshman composition or take tickets at the football game.

Today's man of letters is rarely a free-lance critic like Edmund Wilson or even a part-time academic like Allen Tate. More often he (or she)[4] is a "creative" writer who also does criticism (e.g., John Updike, James Dickey, and—preeminently—Gore Vidal) or a professor who has published his way into the consciousness of the nonacademic literati. Fiedler—along with Alfred Kazin, the late Lionel Trilling, and a few others—represents this latter category. At the level of high culture, such individuals have safe passage between the university and a small part of the professional (or "real") world. Not content with such conventional arrangements, Fiedler has sought to forge a similar passage at the level of popular culture. He has not betrayed academic standards so much as violated the gentleman's agreement that certain borders are not to be crossed, certain gaps not to be closed.

In attempting to assess Fiedler's prodigious achievement, it might be helpful to divide his writings into three broad categories: works of amateur enthusiasm, literary and cultural essays, and book-length ventures in literary anthropology. To my mind the first of these categories—which includes *Being Busted, Freaks,* and Fiedler's various works of fiction and poetry—is most ephemeral. One reads *Being Busted* and *Freaks* not primarily to learn about marijuana laws or human oddities but to see what "Leslie Fiedler" has to say about these subjects. Both are fascinating books, but each seems incomplete. As autobiography, *Being Busted* is too coy and too reticent to reveal what we would most like to know about Fiedler (his refusal to mention any name other than his own I find more irritating than poetic). If anything, *Freaks* suffers from the opposite defect—it gives us too much information and too little analysis. Finally, the fiction and poetry is an uneven mix of the sublime and the ridiculous. Because short fiction seems to be what he does best, his most successful artifacts are to be found in *The Last Jew in America* and *Nude Croquet.* He is a natural raconteur whose truest gifts, as one might expect from his own unique experience, are for depicting alienated Jewish characters and tawdry Western settings.

Although Fiedler has published hundreds of critical articles over the years, those which he thought most worthy of preservation up through 1971 are contained in his two volumes of *Collected Essays.* As Charles R. Larson pointed out at the time, this project was somewhat misleadingly labeled. Not only is the "collected essays" only a selection, but the entire first volume is simply a reprint (photographically reproduced) of *An End to Innocence* and *No! In Thunder.* Because this earlier arrangement has been preserved, essays in the second volume that are thematically related to ones in the first are deprived of what would seem to be logical juxtaposition (e.g., the second volume contains a companion piece to the early essay on the Rosenbergs and two sequels to "Montana; or the End of Jean-Jacques Rousseau"). Moreover, one essay appears word-for-word in both volumes under different titles ("Looking Backward: America from Europe" in volume 1 and "Our Country and Our Culture" in volume 2).[5] From the standpoint of variety and selectivity *A Fiedler Reader* (1977) is a far more satisfying book; however, the *Collected Essays,* for all its editorial flaws, remains an indispensable tool for all serious Fiedler scholars.

The essays in volume 1 have held up remarkably well over the years. In *An End to Innocence* we have those early objects of controversy "Come Back to the Raft Ag'in, Huck Honey!" and "Montana; or the End of Jean-Jacques Rousseau." As important as these essays have been to Fiedler's career, I believe that the arguments he makes here are made with greater clarity and greater subtlety in later works. "Adolescence and Maturity in the American Novel" is an astute bit of literary history; however, the crowning achievement of *An End to Innocence* are the essays on the Hiss case, the Rosenbergs, and Joe McCarthy. That Fiedler's judgments seem so obvious now should not blind us to the fact that at the time most of what was written on these subjects was partisan nonsense. (Charles R. Larson is surely correct in saying "Fiedler has always had a startling ability to analyze real people as if they were characters in books.")[6] If anything, *No! In Thunder* is even better. I doubt that there is another critic in America versatile enough to have written the title essay, "Dante: Green Thoughts in a Green Shade," "The Eye of Innocence," "In the Beginning Was the Word," and "Archetype and Signature."

Although generally less impressive, volume 2 has definite high points and consists almost entirely of material not previously published in book form. The Jewish essays grouped under the heading "To the Gentiles" are themselves a significant contribution to Jewish-American literature. The third section of volume 2—"Cross the Border—Close the Gap"—suffers, particularly in the title essay, from what some might regard as Fiedler's excessive enthusiasm for the counterculture; however, it is redeemed by the brilliantly audacious *"Chutzpah* and *Pudeur."* The middle section, entitled "Unfinished Business," is the longest and least unified in the volume. Nevertheless, it contains several excellent selections, including "Caliban or Hamlet: A Study in Literary Anthropology" and "An Almost Imaginary Interview: Hemingway in Ketchum."

It is in his book-length ventures in literary anthropology that Fiedler has had the greatest opportunity to expand on the insights adumbrated in his essays. He has done so most impressively in *Love and Death in the American Novel.* No doubt, many of the specific criticisms leveled againt this sprawling and cocky tome are justified. (Fiedler himself felt uneasy enough about what he had written in 1960 to put out a revised edition in 1966.) But somehow those criticisms seem beside the point. This book puts forth some exciting and challenging ideas and develops them with the full resources of literary history and critical exegesis. Fiedler's passionate commitment to his subject matter is so infectious that even when we disagree with him he makes us more alive to the possibilities of literature. There is more wisdom in his critical *chutzpah* than in the *pudique* anality of pedants who never venture a generalization for fear that someone may prove them wrong. *Love and Death* is the one book whose scope is most nearly commensurate with Fiedler's extravagant ambitions.

To say that *Love and Death* is Fiedler's best book is also to say that his subsequent works of literary anthropology are less successful. *Waiting for the End* is perhaps better read as a series of essays than as a unified critical treatise. Considered in this light it is a noteworthy, if uneven, achievement. The chapters entitled "The Death of the Old Men," "Traitor or Laureate: The Two Trials of the Poet," and "The Unbroken Tradition" represent Fiedler at his best, while his celebration of such professional barbarians as Allen Ginsberg and William S. Burroughs seems wrongheaded and faddish. As I have suggested earlier, *The Return of the Vanishing American* is so fascinating theoretically that one is disappointed by Fiedler's failure to apply his theories more comprehensively to specific texts. *The Stranger in Shakespeare* does give us plenty of applied criticism and makes us want to reread Shakespeare, if only to see if all earlier discussion of the plays could have missed the mark as badly as Fiedler's analysis would imply. One cannot help but suspect, however, that this book tells us more about Fiedler than about Shakespeare.

This brings us to *What Was Literature?*, a work that merits special notice for two reasons: it contains Fiedler's most recent views on literature, and—if he holds to statements he made to David Gates of *Newsweek*—it will be his last full-length critical book. Structurally, this volume appears to be the arbitrary pairing of a group of short essays on pop literature and a monograph on the "inadvertent epic" (the second section is, in fact, a revised version of just such a monograph published in 1980). The cynic might say that two half books do not necessarily equal one coherent work. Upon closer examination, however, we see that the separate sections of theoretical and practical criticism do shed light on each other. In my judgment, what is seen in this light is worth two cheers.

At the theoretical level, Fiedler is making the same case for the death of canonical literature that he hinted at in "Adolescence and Maturity in the American Novel," that he proclaimed more boldly and explicitly in *Waiting for the End,* and that he gleefully celebrated in *Cross the Border—Close the Gap.* Still, he has never made his case more cogently or more engagingly (perhaps in part because he now realizes more than ever that the counterculture is not the salvation of us all). It is unfortunate, therefore, that he feels constrained to overstate that case and to make *ad hominem* attacks on those who disagree with him. Although technical ineptness may not be the unforgivable sin Fiedler claimed it was in "No! In Thunder," neither is it a matter of inconsequence (at times one gets the impression that he now considers it almost a virtue, a warrant of primitive authenticity). All else being equal, the well-made artifact can generate greater ecstasy than the ill-made one. It is one thing to argue that all else is rarely ever equal, another to denigrate what are perhaps the most sublime poem and novel in the English language (*Paradise Lost* and *Middlemarch*) simply because they are an acquired taste. Nor does it serve the cause of civilized discourse to brand the politically diverse fraternity of "new critics" as Fascists.

The notion of the "inadvertent epic" is valuable because it helps us see how the impact of popular culture on a nation's consciousness can be more complex, even dialectical, than is ordinarily assumed. Fiedler's selection of works in this epic does raise some questions, however. While nearly everyone knows something about *Uncle Tom's Cabin* and *Gone With the Wind,* it is questionable whether *The Birth of a Nation* is of continuing interest to anyone who is not either a cultural historian or a cinema buff. Also, one wonders if enough time has elapsed for us to know whether *Roots* is a pop classic or simply a temporary rage. A television version of Ernest J. Gaines's *The Autobiography of Miss Jane Pittman* drew a record national audience a few years before *Roots,* but Fiedler neglects even to mention it. Nor does he mention Dubose Heyward's *Porgy,* which as novel, play, and Gershwin "folk opera" is perhaps the most mythically powerful portrait of black life yet produced in the twentieth century. It may not fit Fiedler's thematic pattern, but then neither does *Gone With the Wind,* which is primarily the tale of an intraethnic love triangle. All quibbles aside, however, Fiedler's proposals represent a constructive and specific step toward opening up the canon of American literature.

As he was preparing to review Fiedler's *Collected Essays* in 1971, Charles R. Larson had occasion to read several M.A. exams in American literature. Not surprisingly, the critic most frequently cited was Leslie Fiedler (the paper that did not mention him directly simply cribbed his ideas without attribution). Fiedler has always had a special appeal to the young person just beginning to experience the pleasures of literary study (which is not to say that his work fails to challenge even the most erudite). It is as Fiedler himself has noted: "the teacher, that professional amateur, teaches not so much his subject matter as himself. If he is a teacher of literature, he provides for those less experienced in song and story, including the reluctant, the skeptical, the uncooperative, the incompetent, a model of one in whom what seemed dead, mere print on the page, becomes living, a way of life—palpable fulfillment, a transport into the world of wonder" (*WWL,* 114). All of us have known such teachers in the classroom. Fiedler performs the infinitely more difficult task of being one on the printed page. It is for this reason that many members of the rising generation of literary scholars can say that Leslie Fiedler was the critic who made us.[7]

# Notes and References

*Preface*

1. Ronald Bryden, *The Unfinished Hero and Other Essays* (London, 1969), 239.

2. Ralph Waldo Emerson, "Nature," in *Selections from Ralph Waldo Emerson,* edited by Stephen E. Whicher (Boston: Houghton, Mifflin, 1960), 23.

*Chapter One*

1. According to R. Z. Sheppard, he "resembles Karl Marx as portrayed by Richard Dreyfuss" (*Time,* 20 February 1978, 97).

2. See Fiedler's *Being Busted* (New York, 1969), 124; hereafter cited in the text as *BB.* The following abbreviations are used in referring to Fiedler's other books: *Back to China* (New York, 1965), *BC; The Collected Essays of Leslie Fiedler,* 2 vols. (New York, 1971), *CE; A Fiedler Reader* (New York, 1977), *FR; Freaks: Myths and Images of the Secret Self* (New York, 1978), *F; In Dreams Awake: A Historical-Critical Anthology of Science Fiction* (New York, 1975), *I; The Last Jew in America* (New York, 1966), *LJ; Love and Death in the American Novel,* rev. ed. (New York, 1966), *LD; The Messengers Will Come No More* (New York: 1974), *M; Nude Croquet and Other Stories* (New York, 1969), *NC; The Second Stone: A Love Story* (New York, 1963), *SS; The Stranger in Shakespeare* (New York, 1972), *SIS; The Return of the Vanishing American* (New York, 1968), *R; Waiting for the End* (New York, 1964), *WE;* and *What Was Literature?: Class Culture and Mass Society* (New York, 1982), *WWL.*

3. See Benjamin DeMott, "A Talk with Leslie Fiedler," *New York Times Book Review,* 5 March 1978, 9.

4. See John Wakeman, ed., *World Authors 1950–1970* (New York, 1975), 469.

5. Hugh Kenner, "Who Was Leslie Fiedler?," *Harper's,* November 1982, 69.

6. Ronald Bryden, *The Unfinished Hero and Other Essays* (London, 1969), 239–40.

7. See Patricia Ward Biederman, "Leslie Fiedler: The Critic as Outlaw," *Buffalo Courier-Express,* 7 March 1982, 9.

8. Richard Chase, "Leslie Fiedler and American Culture," *Chicago Review,* 14 (Autumn–Winter 1960):10.

9. The biggest internal controversy in which Fiedler was involved while at Montana State was a move (ultimately successful) to depose the

president of the university. When one of Fiedler's allies tried to make a reasoned appeal to an undecided member of the State Board of Education, he was cut short. "Fuck the Good of the University," the lay educator said, "that's like Home and Mother. Who's on your side?" (*BB*, 69).

10. See DeMott, "A Talk," 9.

11. Originally convicted and sentenced to six months in the penitentiary, Fiedler got the New York Court of Appeals to see things his way: " 'The law banning the maintenance of a premises for use of marijuana applies only to a building that the owners specifically maintain for criminal purposes,' said Judge James Gibson for the 5–2 majority. 'It was never contemplated that the criminal taint would attach to a family home should members of the family on one occasion smoke marijuana or hashish there' " ("Being Unbusted," *Time*, 17 July 1972, 50).

12. Biederman, "Leslie Fiedler," 15.

13. Grant Webster, "Leslie Fiedler: Adolescent and Jew as Critic," *Denver Quarterly* 1 (Winter 1967):52.

14. Ibid., 44–45.

15. This, despite the fact that Fiedler has recently gained an unprecedented degree of academic "respectability" by serving on the board of the prestigious English Institute.

16. David Gates, "Fiedler's Utopian Vision," *Newsweek*, 9 January 1984, 11.

17. Ibid.

18. Perhaps part of the answer to this question can be found in Fiedler's favorite epitaph: "He was nothing if not ambivalent."

*Chapter Two*

1. See *WWL*, 14.

2. Because Christian symbolism has lost much of its mythopeic power, explicitly Christian novelists find themselves resorting to the baroque, the grotesque, and—even—the obscene as a means of grabbing the attention of the secular reader. For a discussion of this phenomenon, see Flannery O'Connor, *Mystery and Manners* (New York: Farrar, Straus, & Cudahy, 1962), 154–68; and D. Keith Mano, "Reflections of a Christian Pornographer," *Christianity and Literature* 28 (Spring 1979):5–11.

3. See William K. Wimsatt, Jr., and Cleanth Brooks, *Literary Criticism: A Short History* (New York, 1969), 713.

4. Ibid.

5. Charles R. Larson also points out the duplicity of Wimsatt and Brooks on this issue; however, he finds Fiedler's position suspect on other grounds. "Ultimately," Larson writes, "—and I feel this is the crux of the problem with Fiedler . . . everything becomes a myth, and what started as a serious attempt to define *mythos* and its relationship to poetry—has

grown into a gigantic tumor which Fiedler has used not as an appendage of literature but as literature itself" ("Leslie Fiedler: The Critic and the Myth, the Critic as Myth," *Literary Review* 14 [Winter 1970–71]:141).

6. Wimsatt and Brooks, *Literary Criticism,* 713.

7. Ibid.

8. Cleanth Brooks, "A Note on the Limits of 'History' and the Limits of 'Criticism,' " in *Seventeenth-Century English Poetry: Modern Essays in Criticism,* ed. William R. Keast (New York, 1962), 357.

9. Ibid.

10. Ibid., 358.

*Chapter Three*

1. John Crowe Ransom discusses the masking function of traditional literary forms, and particularly the pastoral elegy, in his essay "A Poem Nearly Anonymous" (in *The World's Body* [Baton Rouge: Louisiana State University Press, 1968], 1–28).

2. See Leo Marx, *The Machine in the Garden* (New York: Oxford University Press, 1964), 34–72.

3. The Good Bad Boy must be at least nominally "wicked" so that he can be redeemed by the Good Good Girl.

4. Fiedler may well feel some affinity for this process. In *What Was Literature?* he writes: "I have graduated, in the view of my critics, from the status of *enfant terrible* to that of 'dirty old man' without passing through a decent maturity" (18–19).

*Chapter Four*

1. This is a somewhat more limited definition of the Gothic than Fiedler had put forth in *Love and Death in the American Novel.* What has happened in recent years is that the older tradition of southern Gothic has given way to a new sunbelt regionalism. As Warren French puts it: "the Ancient Mariner has lost his albatross and has moved into Xanadu, tastefully reconstructed as the latest attraction at Disney World."

2. "Not all Easterns, however, belong in intention or in retrospect to the realm of self-conscious High Art; if any book which deals with the reaction of the American abroad (via tourism or dreams) belongs to the genre, Mark Twain was one of its most assiduous practitioners, all the way from *Innocents Abroad* to *A Connecticut Yankee in King Arthur's Court*" (*R,* 21).

3. In the fifties and sixties James Baldwin wrote fiction of expatriation; however, the racial emphasis of his narratives makes them less Easterns than cosmopolitan Southerns. Even more recently we see a pattern of European/American connections in the work of John Irving. The tradition

of the Northern seems to have been domesticated out of existence, leaving us only with the commuter fiction of Cheever and Updike.

4. Even though evening soaps such as *Dallas* and *Dynasty* are set in the West, their domestic emphases make them non (if not anti) Westerns.

5. Garry Wills, *Bare Ruined Choirs* (Garden City, N.Y.: Doubleday, 1972), 5.

*Chapter Five*

1. See Gates, "Fiedler's Utopian Vision," 11.

2. John Raleigh, "Sex, Sociology and Criticism," *Partisan Review* 27 (Summer 1960):549.

3. Attempts to Americanize the Fielding tradition (e.g., Dos Passos's *USA*) strike us as curiosities or aberrations.

4. Specifically, Rahv says: "When his essay 'Come Back to the Raft Ag'in, Huck Honey,' since become notorious, was printed in *Partisan Review. . . ,* the editors of that magazine thought of it as a talented young man's *jeu d'esprit,* a spoof on academic solemnity, not at all the weighty contribution to the understanding of American letters that Fiedler, who is still pushing its proposition as hard as he can, apparently takes it to be" (*Literature and the Sixth Sense* [Boston, 1969], 399).

5. This dichotomy has almost become a cliché in popular culture. Consider, for example, the characters played by Grace Kelly and Katy Jurado in *High Noon.*

6. Leslie Fiedler, "Second Thoughts on *Love and Death in the American Novel:* My First Gothic Novel," *Novel: A Forum on Fiction* 1 (Fall 1967):11.

*Chapter Six*

1. See Gates, "Fiedler's Utopian Vision," 11.

2. In Faulkner's *Go Down, Moses,* Ike McCaslin seems to believe that there is a fundamental contrast between the purity of interethnic male bonding in the wilderness and the curse of miscegenation that has complicated domestic life in the South.

3. Harriet Beecher Stowe, *Uncle Tom's Cabin* (New York: Signet, 1966), 109.

4. We see similar alternatives in *Wuthering Heights* (Linton and Heathcliff), *Tess of the D'Urbervilles* (Angel and Alec), and a host of other tales.

5. Yes, even white liberals can get in on the act.

*Chapter Seven*

1. Grant Webster, "Leslie Fiedler: Adolescent and Jew as Critic," *Denver Quarterly* 1 (1967):53.

2. When Richard Poirier, chairman of the English Department of Rutgers University, became editor of *Partisan Review* in 1963, the journal began to derive much of its funding from that institution. In 1978, after a messy and acrimonious legal battle, *Partisan Review* moved to Boston University. For a more detailed treatment of the entire history of the journal, see William Phillips, *A Partisan View: Five Decades of the Literary Life* (New York: Stein & Day, 1982).

*Chapter Eight*

1. It seems to me that this is the sort of creative tension that the three unities give to classical tragedy.

2. There have been sporadic attempts during the past three decades to revive the reputation of these nineteenth-century icons. See, for example, George Arms, *The Fields Were Green: A New View of Bryant, Whittier, Holmes, Lowell, and Longfellow* (Stanford: Stanford University Press, 1953) and Robert Penn Warren, *John Greenleaf Whittier's Poetry: An Appraisal and a Selection* (Minneapolis: University of Minnesota Press, 1971).

*Chapter Nine*

1. After the funeral of Jack Kerouac, a group of his old friends and fellow writers (Robert Creeley, Gregory Corso, Allen Ginsberg, et al.) decided "to read poems to one another which turned out to be not their own, not even those of their masters, Whitman or Williams or Pound or Olson, but rather of James Russell Lowell and Henry Wadsworth Longfellow." See Fiedler's "The Children's Hour: or, The Return of the Vanishing Longfellow: Some Reflections on the Future of Poetry," in *Liberations: New Essays on the Humanities in Revolution,* ed. Ihab Hassan (Middletown, Conn.: Wesleyan University Press, 1971), 173.

2. "It is not entirely fortuitous . . . that the only poet writing in English who succeeded in imitating Poe's rhythm and diction with real faithfulness is that composer of nonsense verse for children, Edward Lear" (*WE,* 193).

*Chapter Ten*

1. Kenner, "Who Was Leslie Fiedler?," 69.
2. Ibid., 73.

*Chapter Eleven*

1. See, for example, Garry Wills's "Come Back to the Raft, Will Honey," *National Review,* 1 September 1972, 959, 961.
2. Charles Molesworth, "As a Stranger Give It Welcome," *Nation,* 11 September 1972, 185.

*Chapter Twelve*

1. Because of space limitations, I have chosen not to discuss Fiedler's poetry; however, a good representative sampling can be found in *The Fiedler Reader*, 389–400.

2. Bryden, *Unfinished Hero*, 242.

3. Samuel Irving Bellman, "The American Artist as European Frontiersman: Leslie Fiedler's *The Second Stone*," *Critique: Studies in Modern Fiction* 6 (Winter 1963–64):138.

4. The interethnicity here would be between the Jew Mark and the WASP Clem. In this regard, Bellman notes: "So closely interwoven were the lives of Clem and Mark when they were adolescents that they may well have had at least a latent homosexual relationship" (ibid., 134).

5. Wakeman, *World Authors*, 469.

6. In making precisely this point, Max F. Schulz writes: "Besides his white man's ambivalent feelings of love-hate for the nonwhite races and his desire to atone for Hiroshima, Baro is also portrayed as suffering from arrested development, in search of a mother rather than a wife, and longing to be punished by a hated father" (*Radical Sophistication: Studies in Contemporary Jewish-American Novelists* [Athens, Ohio, 1969], 167).

7. This is, of course, an ironic allusion to Hemingway's story "Fathers and Sons," in which the protagonist remembers his initiation into sex with an Indian girl ("she did first what no one has ever done better").

*Chapter Thirteen*

1. Chase, "Leslie Fiedler," 16–17.

2. Bryden, "My Son," 240.

3. See George H. Nash, *The Conservative Intellectual Movement in America Since 1945* (New York: Basic Books, 1976), 112.

4. Although Fiedler mentions no names, the case sounds very much like that of Willmoore Kendall and Yale.

5. See Alison Lurie, "To the Sideshow," *New York Review of Books*, 23 March 1978.

6. There is also Donald Davidson's *Caught Short* (1972), the true story of a dwarf who started out as bat boy for the Boston Braves and had worked his way up to a front office position by the time the team had moved (via Milwaukee) to Atlanta. Another surprising omission is Fiedler's failure to mention Teilhard de Chardin in his chapter on superhuman mutation. Finally, if a revised version of the book is ever prepared, one would expect to see some discussion of Bernard Pomerance's 1981 play *The Elephant Man*. The staging of that play, without makeup for the actor playing the Elephant Man, is certainly consistent with Fiedler's notion of freaks as images of the self.

*Chapter Fourteen*

1. See, for example, Walter K. Gordon, ed., *Literature in Critical Perspectives* (New York: Appleton-Century-Crofts, 1968); Wilbur Scott, ed., *Five Approaches of Literary Criticism* (New York: Macmillan, 1962); and Walter Sutton, *Modern American Criticism* (Englewood Cliffs, N.J.: Prentice-Hall, 1963).

2. The moral approach itself has never entirely disappeared. For a notable recent example, see John Gardner, *On Moral Fiction* (New York: Basic Books, 1978).

3. See Biederman, "Leslie Fiedler," 11.

4. As I am using it, the concept "man of letters" is sufficiently generic to include such women as Elizabeth Hardwick and Mary McCarthy and (among a younger generation) Joyce Carol Oates and Diane Johnson.

5. Let me hasten to acknowledge that all of these points are made in Charles R. Larson's "The Good Bad Boy and Guru of American Letters," *Saturday Review,* 25 December 1971, 27–28, 35.

6. Ibid., 27–28.

7. I borrow this term from the *Sewanee Review,* which has run a series under the title "The Critics Who Made Us."

# Selected Bibliography

PRIMARY SOURCES

1. Criticism

*The Collected Essays of Leslie Fiedler.* 2 vols. New York: Stein & Day, 1971.
*Cross the Border, Close the Gap.* New York: Stein & Day, 1972.
*An End to Innocence: Essays on Culture and Politics.* Boston: Beacon Press, 1955.
*The Inadvertent Epic: From "Uncle Tom's Cabin" to "Roots."* New York: Simon & Schuster, 1980.
*The Jew in the American Novel.* New York: Herzl Press, 1959.
*Love and Death in the American Novel.* New York: Criterion Books, 1960; rev. ed. New York: Stein & Day, 1966.
*No! In Thunder: Essays on Myth in Literature.* Boston: Beacon Press, 1960.
*Olaf Stapledon: A Man Divided.* New York: Oxford University Press, 1983.
*The Return of the Vanishing American.* New York: Stein & Day, 1968.
*The Stranger in Shakespeare.* New York: Stein & Day, 1972.
*To the Gentiles.* New York: Stein & Day, 1972.
*Unfinished Business.* New York: Stein & Day, 1972.
*Waiting for the End.* New York: Stein & Day, 1964.
*What Was Literature?: Class Culture and Mass Society.* New York: Simon & Schuster, 1982.

2. Fiction

*Back to China.* New York: Stein & Day, 1965.
*The Last Jew in America.* New York: Stein & Day, 1966.
*The Messengers Will Come No More.* New York: Stein & Day, 1974.
*Nude Croquet and Other Stories.* New York: Stein & Day, 1969.
*Pull Down Vanity and Other Stories.* Philadelphia: Lippincott, 1962.
*The Second Stone: A Love Story.* New York: Stein & Day, 1963.

3. Other Nonfiction

*Being Busted.* New York: Stein & Day, 1969.
*A Fiedler Reader.* New York: Stein & Day, 1977.
*Freaks: Myths and Images of the Secret Self.* New York: Simon & Schuster, 1978.

4. Works Edited by Fiedler

*The Art of the Essay.* New York: Crowell, 1958.

*The Continuing Debate: Essays on Education.* Edited with Jacob Vincour. New York: Saint Martin's Press, 1964.

*English Literature: Opening Up the Canon.* Edited with Houston A. Baker, Jr. Baltimore: Johns Hopkins University Press, 1981.

*In Dreams Awake: A Historical-Critical Anthology of Science Fiction.* New York: Dell, 1975.

*The Master of Ballantrae,* by Robert Louis Stevenson. New York: Rinehart, 1954.

*O Brave New World: American Literature from 1600 to 1840.* Edited with Arthur Zeiger. New York: Dell, 1968.

*Whitman: Selections from "Leaves of Grass."* New York: Dell, 1959.

## SECONDARY SOURCES

1. Biography and General Criticism

Biederman, Patricia Ward. "Leslie Fiedler: The Critic as Outlaw." *Buffalo Courier-Express,* 7 March 1982, 9–11, 13–15. An unusually intelligent Sunday supplement feature based on an interview with Fiedler just prior to the publication of *What Was Literature?*.

Borklund, Elmer. *Contemporary Literary Critics.* Detroit: Gale Research Company, 1982, pp. 207–11. A general discussion of Fiedler's career up through the early 1980s: "Critics who assume the role of oracle are in a difficult position: they have to be right. But if they are confident of their vision. . . , they apparently feel that humble matters of argument and proof can be left to the faithful."

Dembo, L. S. "Dissent and Dissent: A Look at Fiedler and Trilling." In *Contemporary American-Jewish Literature: Critical Essays,* edited by Irving Malin, 134–55. Bloomington: Indiana University Press, 1973. A general discussion of Fiedler's thought through the early 1970s.

DeMott, Benjamin. "A Talk with Leslie Fiedler." *New York Times Book Review,* 5 March 1978, 9, 36. A wide-ranging interview conducted at the time that *Freaks* was published.

Gates, David. "Fiedler's Utopian Vision." *Newsweek,* 9 January 1984, 11. A biographical update based on an interview with Fiedler in late 1983.

Goldsmith, Arnold L. *American Literary Criticism: 1905–1965.* Boston: Twayne, 1979, pp. 151–59. Surveys Fiedler's career up through the mid-1960s: "The most controversial of all the Myth Critics, and the most important."

**Larson, Charles R.** "Leslie Fiedler: The Critic and the Myth, the Critic as Myth." *Literary Review* 14 (Winter 1970–71):133–43. A discussion of Fiedler's concept of myth: "Fiedler's criticism remains for the most part highly readable and almost uniformly fresh—whether one agrees with what he says or not."

**Wakeman, John,** ed. *World Authors 1950–1970.* New York: H. H. Wilson Co., 1975, pp. 468–71. A general summary of Fiedler's career up through 1972. Contains autobiographical statement of about 2,000 words.

**Webster, Grant.** "Leslie Fiedler: Adolescent and Jew as Critic." *Denver Quarterly* 1 (Winter 1967):44–53. An intemperate attack on Fiedler's achievement through the mid-1960s: "it is relatively easy to judge Fiedler philosophically, for his writings are dominated by a single theme: a rage at the loss of a patriarchal system of values and the consequent condemnation of modern American culture."

**Widmer, Kingsley.** *The Literary Rebel.* Carbondale: Southern Illinois University Press, 1965, pp. 160–64. Sees Fiedler as a rebel manqué, "always so skittishly and anxiously *au courant.*"

## 2. On Specific Works

**Aldiss, Brian.** "In Orbit with the Star Maker." *Times Literary Supplement,* 23 September 1983, 1007–8. Favorable review of *Olaf Stapledon.* Credits Fiedler with helping to rekindle interest in Stapledon.

**Aldridge, John W.** *Time to Murder and Create: The Contemporary Novel in Crisis.* New York: David McKay, 1966, pp. 225–29. A negative review of *The Second Stone:* "Clem and Mark Stone have now joined the distinguished company of Natty Bumppo and Chingachgook, Ishmael and Queequeg, and Huck and Jim to show that love between men and women is a snare and delusion, and that the real thing is reserved for us boys all alone together out there on that raft."

**Alter, Robert.** "Jewish Dreams and Nightmares." In Malin, pp. 58–77. An attack on "Master of Dreams": Fiedler "clearly shares with the medieval Midrash an indifference to historical perspective which allows him to speak of the varied literary productions of far-flung times and places as one eternal system."

———. Review of *The Messengers Will Come No More. New York Times Book Review,* 29 September 1974, 5–6. "[T]he fiction as it is concocted seems too often a theological joke without a point, or one that takes itself too seriously, or, still worse, a joke stitched together from threadbare materials, trying to simulate novelty chiefly through the aggressiveness of its bad taste."

**Bellman, Samuel Irving.** "The American Artist as European Frontiersman: Leslie Fiedler's *The Second Stone.*" *Critique: Studies in Modern Fiction* 6

(Winter 1963–64):131–43. "[A] remarkable embodiment in fictional form of Fiedler's criticisms, analyses, mythographic projections, and quasi-historical interpretations of our Western cultural heritage."
————. "In Groups Within Groups." *Saturday Review,* 30 July 1966, 31–32. A tasteless hatchet job on *The Last Jew in America:* "Mere stereotypes and anti-stereotypes don't make good stories."

Brooks, Cleanth. "A Note on the Limits of 'History' and the Limits of 'Criticism.' " *Seventeenth-Century English Poetry: Modern Essays in Criticism,* edited by William R. Keast, 352–58. New York: Oxford University Press, 1962. In his defense of formalist criticism, Brooks argues that myth critics such as Fiedler and traditional scholars such as Douglas Bush are really opposite sides of the same coin, in that both disregard the limits and integrity of literature.

Bryden, Ronald. "My Son the Frontiersman." In *The Unfinished Hero and Other Essays.* London: Faber & Faber, 1969, pp. 239–42. An unusually discerning and not unfavorable review of *Pull Down Vanity and Other Stories:* "It is no accident that Mr. Fiedler's title comes from Pound's *Cantos.* His stance, too, is that of the bawdy, bearded Western prophet."

Chase, Richard. "Leslie Fiedler and American Culture." *Chicago Review* 14 (Autumn–Winter 1960):8–18. A long, mostly negative, review-essay on *Love and Death in the American Novel:* "The American novel is not merely a chronicle of nihilistic despair titillated up with a misplaced eroticism."

Daniels, Guy. "The Sorrows of Baro Finkelstone." *New Republic,* 22 May 1965, 25–27. A snide and inaccurate review of *Back to China:* It "is, in today's sterile jargon, an 'anti-anti comic novel'—in short, literary Pop Art. Fiedler is nothing if not fashionable."

DeMott, Benjamin. "The Negative American." In *Hells and Benefits: A Report on American Minds, Matters, and Possibilities.* New York: Basic Books, 1962, pp. 193–205. A favorable review-essay on *Love and Death in the American Novel:* "far from an outrage, it is, in truth, one of the very few important assessments of our culture to appear since the publication . . . of Matthiessen's *American Renaissance.* "

Goodman, Walter. "The Professor and the Police." *Commentary,* March 1970, 85–88. A generally positive review of *Being Busted:* "an engagingly discursive book. . . . Fiedler conveys a strong sense of place and period."

Kazin, Alfred. "Honoring the Dark Impulse." *Atlantic,* January 1983, 92–93, 96. A mildly negative review of *What Was Literature?:* Fiedler "has a regrettable way of lining up classics and commercials, Dickens and Edgar Rice Burroughs, Shakespearean theater and TV."

**Kenner, Hugh.** "Who Was Leslie Fiedler?" *Harper's,* November 1982, 69–73. A thoughtful, erudite review-essay on *What Was Literature?.* Not nearly as negative as its headline caption: "the battle continues between literature and the man who wants it dead."

**Kermode, Frank.** "Modernisms." In *Innovations: Essays on Art and Ideas,* edited by Bernard Bergonzi, 66–92. London: Macmillan, 1968. Devotes a couple of pages to discussing Fiedler's "The New Mutants."

**Krim, Seymour.** "*Waiting for the End:* Leslie Fiedler's Bronco Ride from Pocahontas to Marjorie Morningstar." In *Shake It for the World, Smartass.* New York: Dial Press, 1970, pp. 43–51. Despite his admiration for Fiedler, Krim sees him as too elitist and insufficiently attentive to popular culture!

**Kristol, Irving.** "A Traitor to His Class?" *Kenyon Review* 22 (Summer 1960):505–9. A favorable review of *Love and Death in the American Novel:* "The comparison it inevitably brings to mind is with D. H. Lawrence's *Studies in Classic American Literature.* . . . I think Fiedler's book is the superior of the two."

**Lander, Dawn.** "Eve Among the Indians." *The Authority of Experience,* edited by Arlyn Diamond and Lee R. Edwards, 194–211. Amherst: University of Massachusetts Press, 1977. A feminist attack on *The Return of the Vanishing American.*

**Larson, Charles R.** "The Good Bad Boy and Guru of American Letters." *Saturday Review,* 25 December 1971, 27–28, 35. An extremely perceptive and generally favorable review of the *Collected Essays:* "Fiedler has become what he set out to be: a living myth, a part of his criticism itself."

**Lewis, R. W. B.** "Gothic Criticism and American Fiction." *Yale Review* 49 (Summer 1960):610–14. "[T]he perspective [of *Love and Death in the American Novel* ] is fresh and what Mr. Fiedler says by means of it is memorable. He is one of the few literary critics of his generation whose ideas one can actually remember."

**Lurie, Alison.** "To the Sideshow." *New York Review of Books,* 23 March 1978, 22, 24. Commenting on *Freaks* and *A Fiedler Reader:* Fiedler's "long literary career, though marked with bursts of great brilliance and remarkable insights of which most critics would be incapable, has also been marred by overstatement, restlessness, and egotism."

**Molesworth, Charles.** "As a Stranger Give It Welcome." *Nation,* 11 September 1972, 183–85. An extremely positive review of *The Stranger in Shakespeare;* finds Fiedler's idiosyncratic readings to be "brilliant" and praises him for having the courage to "talk about [himself] apropos of Shakespeare."

**Rahv, Philip.** "The Critic as *Littérateur:* Leslie Fiedler and John Aldridge." In *Literature and the Sixth Sense.* Boston: Houghton Mifflin, 1969, pp. 398–408. A carping attack on Fiedler posing as a review of *Waiting for the End.*

Rexroth, Kenneth. "Ids and Animuses." *New York Times Book Review,* 17 March 1968, 4, 47. A negative review of *The Return of the Vanishing American:* "Ultimately Fiedler's distortion of vision derives from his membership in a small circle of extremely ethnocentric people—the self-styled New York Establishment."

Ricks, Christopher. "I Contain Mobs." *New Republic,* 20 December 1982, 30–33. Negative review of *What Was Literature?:* "On every important matter in this book, Fiedler is in contradiction with himself."

Rosenberg, Harold. "Couch Liberalism and the Guilty Past." In *The Tradition of the New.* New York: Grove Press, 1961, pp. 221–40. An attack on the political essays in *An End to Innocence:* "Fiedler's line is: We have been guilty of being innocent. Only by confessing will we terminate our culpability."

Sale, Roger. *On Not Being Good Enough: Writings of a Working Critic.* New York: Oxford University Press, 1979, pp. 144–48. A mixed review of the *Collected Essays:* Fiedler is "always putting himself into situations where he is speaking against this fashion or that obsolescence, deriding some official line, jockeying for some new position."

Schulz, Max F. "Leslie A. Fiedler and the Hieroglyphs of Life." In *Radical Sophistication: Studies in Contemporary Jewish-American Novelists.* Athens: Ohio University Press, 1969, pp. 154–72. Discusses Fiedler's first three novels: "Fiedler's bumptious personality will not let him peer very far into the abyss before his ironic contemporary mood diverts him into cool laughter."

Sheppard, R. Z. "Leslie Fiedler's Monster Party." *Time,* 20 February 1978, 95–96. Positive review of *Freaks:* "a combination sideshow, meditation on human nature and medical textbook of the sort that librarians once kept locked away with scandalous volumes like Krafft-Ebbing's *Psychopathia Sexualis.*"

Simon, John. "Leslie Fiedler or How to End a Dull Party." In *Acid Test.* New York: Stein & Day, 1963, pp. 280–85. A rave review of *No! In Thunder:* "I consider Mr. Fiedler the most amusing, most challenging, most delectably readable of our critics."

Sutton, Walter. *Modern American Criticism.* Englewood Cliffs, N.J.: Prentice Hall, 1963, pp. 211–15. Essentially a discussion of *Love and Death in the American Novel:* "His bold use of psychological concepts leads to fresh insights. However, Fiedler's archetypal pattern is Procrustean."

Vidal, Gore. "The Hacks of Academe." In *Matters of Fact and Fiction: Essays 1973–1976.* New York: Random House, 1977, pp. 89–98. In response to Fiedler's "The Death and Rebirth of the Novel":

"America's liveliest full-time professor and seducer of the *Zeit-geist*. . . , a redskin most at home in white clown makeup. . . . He can actually see what is in front of him and this is what makes him such a useful figure."

**Wills, Garry.** "Come Back to the Raft, Will Honey." *National Review*, 1 September 1972, 959, 961. A negative review of *The Stranger in Shakespeare:* Fiedler's "drearily familiar 'archetypes'—the castrating woman, the menacing dark man, the savage . . . become less convincing the more they are made to explain."

**Wimsatt, William K., Jr., and Brooks, Cleanth.** *Literary Criticism: A Short History.* New York: Alfred A. Knopf, 1964, pp. 712–14. Argues that in "Archetype and Signature" "Fiedler is engaged in reasserting a full dualism" of literary form and content.

# Index

**DATE DUE**

| | | | |
|---|---|---|---|
| | | | |
| | | | |
| | | | |
| | | | |
| | | | |
| | | | |
| | | | |
| | | | |
| | | | |
| | | | |
| | | | |
| | | | |
| | | | |
| | | | |
| | | | |
| | | | |
| | | | |
| | | | |
| | | | |
| | | | |
| GAYLORD | | | PRINTED IN U.S.A. |